*Ādi Śaṅkarācārya's*

# Aparokṣānubhūti

Adventure of Consciousness

4

- Analytical Ayurveda/ Dr. K A Latheef
- Upanisads and Edith Stein: *A Dialogue on Models of The Person*/ Thomas Marottipparayil
- Tīrthaṅkarāsana: *A Work on Jaina Yoga*/ Shantilal D. Parakh
- Aparokṣānubhūti: *The Essence of Self Realization*/ Dr. Shrikrishna Deshmukh

*Ādi Śaṅkarācārya's*

# Aparokṣānubhūti

DR. SHRIKRISHNA DESHMUKH

*The Essence of Self Realization*

*Translated by*
MUKTA WALVEKAR

MOTILAL BANARSIDASS PUBLICATIONS

Aparokṣānubhūti/ Dr. Shrikrishna Deshmukh

**First Edition : Delhi, 2019**

ISBN : 978 81 940111 7 0



*Also available at*

MOTILAL BANARSIDASS PUBLICATIONS
41 U.A. Bungalow Road, Jawahar Nagar, Delhi 110 007
1 B, J.S. Compound, Kennedy Bridge, Nana Chowk, Mumbai 400 007
203 Royapettah High Road, Mylapore, Chennai 600 004
49, 8th F Main III Block, Jayanagar, Bengaluru 560 011

**MLBD Cataloguing-in-Publication Data**
[illegible] *of Self Realization*
by Dr. Shrikrishna Deshmukh
ISBN : 978 81 940111 7 0
I. Acknowlegement II. Introdution III. Contents

*Published by*
Motilal Banarsidass Publications
*mlbdbooks@gmail.com*
*Printed by* Replika Press Pvt. Ltd

# Ādi Śaṅkarācārya

## ~ The Foremost Exponent of Advaita Vedānta ~

(788- 820 CE, Kaladi, Kerala)

# Acknowledgement

Aparokṣānubhūti is an acclaimed ancient treatise that uniquely presents the Asṭāṅgayoga practices in the light of Advaita Vedānta. It has been perhaps the most involving and gratifying journey for me to work on the translation of this exceptional commentary. I feel enriched and evolved, like never before.

Many people made a selfless, earnest contribution in this process. Dr. Jyotsna Patankar and Mrs. Irina Derwall took painstaking efforts for proofreading the translation. Mrs. Sonali Phadke worked diligently on the beautiful, perceptive cover design. My husband, Pramod Walvekar designed the book by paying attention to all minute nuances. My family has been extremely supportive throughout the period of translation of this book. My sincere thanks to all of them!

My revered Sadguru **Dr. Shrikrishna Deshmukh** has been a pillar of support in this arduous journey. I am deeply indebted to him for everything in life. This translation is only a result of his priceless guidance, blessings, and supreme grace!

**Mrs. Mukta Walvekar**
(Translator)

# Introduction

The insightful compositions authored by Ādi Śaṅkarācārya are based on the doctrine of Advaita Vedānta. However, each composition emphasizes a different aspect each time and presents the same philosophy in a distinct, unique and perceptive manner. Readers can feel the joy in learning new subtleties and approaches in each text. The treatise of Aparokṣānubhūti consists of 144 verses, which makes it just the right size for the students of Vedānta. The text explains the fundamental principle, Sat-Cit-Ānanda (Brahman), in a discerning manner. It also unfolds various spiritual practices for liberation (Mokṣa), obstacles in the path of liberation and ways to remove them. Ācārya has not only explained theoretical aspects of Vedānta, but also outlined a systematic path to attain Self-realization in this incisive text.

Spiritual pursuit can be of three kinds -

- Core principles of the philosophy (*Siddhāntābhimukha*, सिद्धान्ताभिमुख)
- Spiritual practices for Self-realization (*Sādhanābhimukha*, साधनाभिमुख)
- Application of the philosophy in day-to-day life (*Jīvanābhimukha*, जीवनाभिमुख)

Aparokṣānubhūti clearly calls attention to the first two aspects. E.g. in the very first invocatory verse, the author specifically cites that Īśvara is the creator of 14 esoteric planes (7 Swarga Loka, 7 Pātāla Loka). On one hand, Vedānta presents the theory of no-origination (Ajātavāda), which states that the empirical world has no real origin, birth or existence. Alternatively, Vedānta also states that everything in the world is verily Brahman (Sarva Brahmavāda). Despite these theories, why has the author mentioned 14 esoteric planes in the very first verse of this treatise? This is because most people believe that the world is real with all its diversities. So, to support the common mass faith in Īśvara, Ācārya has used the language of Adhyāropa, which states that Īśvara is the creator of this world. It is a recommended practice to teach Vedānta in a gradual, evolving manner to ordinary seekers. Ācārya clearly maintains the following approach in his treatise -

**अध्यारोप अपवादाभ्यां निष्प्रपञ्चं प्रपञ्च्यते ।**
**शिष्याणां बोधसिद्ध्यर्थं तत्त्वज्ञैः कल्पितः क्रमः ॥**

*Adhyāropa Apavādābhyāṁ niṣprapañcaṁ prapñcyate /*
*Śiṣyaṇāṁ bodhasiddhyarthaṁ tattvajñaiḥ kalpitaḥ kramaḥ //*

Māṇḍūkya Karika explains Asparśayoga (अस्पर्शयोग), which states that Brahman does not touch anything else. [The world does not exist as per Ajātavāda; hence Brahman cannot touch it.] But even then, millions of people believe that the world exists for real. Therefore, for the convenience of masses, Vedānta first accepts the existence of the world as real, which is called as 'false attribution' (**Adhyāropa**, अध्यारोप). Later it explains the theory of One, non-dual

Brahman, and refutes the existence of the world, which was earlier accepted as real. This is called as **Apavāda** (अपवाद). With this approach, Vedānta delicately leads ordinary seekers from the gross world to the subtle principle of Brahman.

To explain this in more detail, Vedānta states the concept of Vivarta (विवर्त). Vivarta is an 'imaginary change' where the perceived object (the world) appears to be different from its substratum (Brahman) - both visually and in essence. As a result of Vivarta, Brahman is completely hidden and cannot be known. Names and forms conceal Brahman. The world is but an illusive appearance. Vedānta accepts the world as real (Adhyāropa) initially, and later refutes the existence of the world (Apavāda).

Before we study this treatise, it is important to clarify a few terms right at the outset. The word **Aparokṣa Jñāna**, (अपरोक्ष ज्ञान) means 'direct realization of Brahman as the real Self'. The word **Parokṣa Jñāna** (परोक्ष ज्ञान) means **Indirect** knowledge that is theoretical, empirical, connotative, or deductive in nature. Parokṣa Jñāna can be attained by reading, listening or inferencing. Katha Upaniṣad states -

**नायमात्मा प्रवचनेन लभ्यो न मेधया न बहुधा श्रुतेन ।**

*Nayamātmā pravacanen labhyo*
*na medhayā na bahudhā śruten / (1.1.23)*

- Ātman can neither be realized by listening to spiritual discourses nor by studying Vedas nor by the intellect.

Aparokṣānubhūti of Brahman cannot be attained with the help of the five senses, or the nine epistemical means of gaining knowledge (Pramāṇa) such as perception, inference, analogy etc. Hence Brahman is called as 'Self-cognizant' (Swasamvedya, स्वसंवेद्य).

Bṛhadāraṇyaka Upaniṣad states -

**यत्सक्षात् अपरोक्षात् ब्रह्म ।**

*Yat sakṣāt aparokṣat Brahman / (3.4.1)*

- Brahman is openly evident and direct. (It can be realized only by being One with it).

It is difficult to learn, accept and assimilate this fact quickly in the beginning. The word Sākṣātkāra (साक्षात्कार) typically indicates the process of seeing the live form of a deity during meditation. However, the actual meaning of Sākṣātkāra is being One with the object of meditation. Lord Kṛṣṇa says the same in Bhagvad-Gītā -

**प्रत्यक्षावगमम् ।**

*Pratyakṣāvagamaṁ / (9.2)*

- (This knowledge of Brahman can only be attained) by direct realization.

Aparokṣānubhūti is the only real way to experience JīvaBrahmaikya - the union of Jīva with Brahman (individual Consciousness with Pure Consciousness). People, who are oblivious to this fact, perform various other spiritual practices and traditional rituals like worship, fasting, pious observances (Vrata, व्रत), reading scriptures, going on pilgrimages, or singing holy songs (Bhajana, भजन). Rituals have a definite value in spiritual pursuit. Some people even mistakenly think that Bhagvad-Gītā mainly propounds Karmayoga (path of action), and wrongly believe that the ultimate Knowledge of Brahman is just one facet of Karmayoga. Such is the impact of the path of action and worship on the mindset of ordinary people. However, Katha Upaniṣad states -

न हि अध्रुवैः प्राप्यते हि ध्रुवं तत् ।

*Na hi adhṛvaiḥ prāpyate hi dhṛvaṁ tat / (1.2.10)*

- The eternal principle cannot be attained with the help of non-eternal practices.

All rituals mentioned above are ultimately actions, which begin and end. Brahman is beginingless, endless, vast, all-pervasive, and that which cannot be created or produced by anything. No action can lead to the Knowledge of Brahman. Anything that is produced or created gets destroyed in the due course of time. Brahman is birthless, deathless, transcendental and eternal. Hence, human mind cannot grasp it with the intellect, like any other routine knowledge.

Every spiritual practice is insentient. Sentient Jīva performs the spiritual practice, so sometimes the practice itself is perceived as sentient. Chanting, meditation, yoga are all insentient practices, which begin and end eventually. They are performed by sentient Jīva. St. Tukārāma says -

बोलावा विठ्ठल पाहावा विठ्ठल, करावा विठ्ठल जीवभाव ॥

*Bolāvā Vitthala pāhāvā Vitthala, karāvā Vitthala Jīvabhāva //*

- Jīva should chant the Mantra of Vitthala, watch Him lovingly, and be One with Brahman while doing so.

This insightful Abhanga (a type of devotional poetry) says that the union of Jīva and Brahman should take place automatically while watching the deity and chanting the Mantra of Vitthala. In fact, Jīva is already One with Brahman. Their union cannot be achieved per say. The very nature of Jīva is Brahman. However, Jīva delusively feels he is separate from Brahman. This is only due to ignorance (Ajñāna, अज्ञान). The ignorance is eradicated in the process of watching the deity with unselfish love, devotion, and chanting earnestly His Mantra. As a result, the real Self (Ātman) is revealed as is. Jīva does not gain the Knowledge of Ātman. Ātman itself is Absolute, Pure Knowledge. When Jīva disappears in Ātman, no separate knower is left who can know Ātman. One needs to understand this delicate subtlety in the process of Self-realization. Ātman is non-doer (Akartā, अकर्ता). Jīva, who is the doer (Kartā, कर्ता) cannot be One with the non-doer Ātman as long as Jīva considers himself as a separate practitioner or seeker.

Bṛhadāraṇyaka Upaniṣad states this fact in many verses. Seekers should delve deep into them.

**यः पृथिव्यां तिष्ठन् पृथिव्या अन्तरो यं पृथिवी न वेद यस्य पृथिवी शरीरं यः पृथिवीमन्तरो यमयत्येष शरीरं यः पृथिवीमन्तरो यमयत्येष त आत्मान्तर्याम्यमृतः ॥**

*Yah Pṛthivyām tiṣṭhan Pṛthivyā antaro yaṁ Pṛthivi na veda yasya Pṛthivi śariraṁ yah Pṛthivimantaro yamayatyesha śariraṁ yah Pṛthivimantaro yamayatyeṣa ta Ātmāntaryāmyamṛtah || (3.7.3)*

- He inhabits the earth and is also within it, however the earth does not know Him. The earth is His body, and He governs the earth from within. He is the immortal Self, who controls you (each Jiva) from within.

The Upaniṣad further states the same fact about water, fire, wind, sky, sun, direction (quarter), moon, stars, Prāṇa, Vāṇī (speech), eyes etc.

The second verse in Bṛhadāraṇyaka Upaniṣad is -

**यद्वैतन्न जिघ्रति जिघ्रन्वै तन्न जिघ्रति न हि घ्रातुर्घ्रातेर्विपरिलोपो विद्यतेऽविनाशित्वान् न तु तद्द्वितीयमस्ति ततोऽन्यद्विभक्तं यज्जिघ्रेत् ॥**

*Yadvaitanna jighrati jighranvai tanna jighrati na hi ghrāturghrāterviparilopo vidyate'vināśitvān na tu taddvitīyamasti tato'nyadvibhaktaṁ yajjighret || (4.3.24)*

\- One who does not smell, although smelling, he does not smell. The smeller's power of smelling can never be lost, because it is immortal. In this state, there is no other thing separate from him, which he can smell.

The Upaniṣad further describes the same fact about tasting, speaking, hearing, knowing etc.

These verses imply that Ātman pervades the five great elements (Pañcamahābhūta) as well as the five senses and regulates them. Yet, the senses cannot comprehend Ātman. In reality, nothing else exists other than the One, non-dual, non-differential (Bhedaśūnya) Ātman. So, how can one possibly know Ātman separately from himself?

The theory of quintuplication (Pañcīkaraṇa) is another approach to learn this same fact. Vedānta states that the intellect (Buddhi) is made of the 'fire element' (Agnitattva). The fire cannot comprehend Ātman since fire is insentient. So, the intellect created from the fire element cannot comprehend Ātman as well. Similarly, the insentient 'wind element' cannot realize Ātman; so, the mind (Manas, मन) made up from the wind cannot comprehend Ātman as well. The teachings of Gītā and Upaniṣad can be learnt better in this light.

Lord Kṛṣṇa says in Bhagvad-Gītā -

योो बुद्धेः परतस्तु सः ।

*Yo buddheḥ paratastu saḥ / (3.42)*

- Ātman (Pure Consciousness) is subtler than the intellect and beyond the capacity of the intellect, so it cannot be realized by the intellect.

Kena Upaniṣad says -

यन्मनुसा न मनुते ।

*Yanmanusā na manute / (1.5)*

- (Ātman is the one that) cannot be comprehended by the mind (but by which the mind is comprehended).

Another verse in Kena Upaniṣad states -

न विद्मो न विजानीमो यथैतदनुशिष्यात् अन्यदेव तद्विदितादथो अविदितादधि ।

*Na vidmo na vijanīmo yathaitadanushiśyāt anyadeva tadviditādatho aviditādadhi / (1.1.3)*

- (Sadguru says -) We do not know how to describe it (Ātman). It is different from what is known and beyond what is unknown.

The ancient era belonged to such eminent Sadgurus, who openly accepted that they do not know Ātman, nor can they describe it nor talk about it, and disciples who nurtured unwavering faith in their Masters despite them saying so.

Vedānta and the treatises written by the enlightened saints are replete with verses that help us better understand the nature of Aparokṣānubhūti of Ātman.

Some of them are as follows –

1. ॐ नमोजी आद्या । वेद प्रतिपाद्या । जय जय स्वसंवेद्या । आत्मरूपा ॥

*Om namoji ādyā / Veda pratipādyā /*

*Jaya jaya Swasamvedyā / Ātmarūpā // (Jñāneśwarī 1.1)*

- Ātman is primordial, Self-cognizant and expounded in Vedas.

This verse is the very crux of the treatise of Jñāneśwarī, which is a magnificent commentary on Bhagvad-Gītā in Marāthi. It says that Ātman is the most primordial principle. Nothing has existed before Ātman. **Ādya** (आद्य) in this verse indicates that Ātman is beginningless, birthless, deathless, eternal and the ultimate Truth (Anadi, Nitya, Aja, Amara, Satya; अनादि, अज, अमर, नित्य, सत्य). **Veda pratipādyā** (वेद प्रतिपाद्या) indicates that Ātman is as described in Vedas. **Swasamvedyā** (स्वसंवेद्या) indicates that Ātman is Self-cognizant, which means it can be realized only by being One with it.

2. जडाजडीं अंशीं । राहाटे जे सरिसी । ते चेतना गा तुजसी । लटिकें नाहीं ॥

*Jaḍājaḍī aṅshī / Rāhāṭe je sarisī /*

*Te Cetanā gā tujasī / Laṭike nāhī // (Jñā.13. 137)*

जे सर्वत्र सदा सम । तेथ विभाग अधमोत्तम । मतिवशें संभ्रम । विवंचिती ॥

*Je sarvatra sadā sama / Tetha vibhāga adhamottama /*

*Mativaśe saṁbhrama / Vivañciti // (Jñā. 4.70)*

- The universe is divided into sentient and insentient entities. These verses state that Brahman pervades both types of entities equally, everywhere and at all times.

Brahman pervades through all of them. It is not the case that Brahman is present in one place and absent in the other (Sarvatra, सर्वत्र). It is also not the case that it is less in one place and more in the other (Sama, सम). It transcends time. In other words, it is present in the past, the present and the future (Sada, सदा). The vastness and all-pervasiveness of Brahman has no differentiation of any kind. Only the deluded human mind perceives it to have differentiation.

3. Brahman is neither objective nor subjective. Objective knowledge is descriptive, while subjective knowledge is reflective. However, Brahman is not an 'element' so it cannot be described or reflected upon.

4. In a Sanskrit treatise named Dṛk-Dṛśya Viveka, it is stated that 'Draṣṭā (perceiver) perceives Dṛśya (objects) in the light of Dṛk (Ātman)'. Here Dṛk is sentient and illuminor (Prakāśaka), while Dṛśya is insentient and illumined (Prakāśya). Dṛk illumines everything that is perceivable (knowable). Even then, one can better understand Dṛk with the help of Dṛśya.

Kena Upaniṣad clearly explains the same principle -

**प्रतिबोध विदितं मतं अमृतत्वं हि विन्दते ।**

*Pratibodha viditaṁ mataṁ amṛtatvaṁ hi vindate / (2.4)*

- Every 'acquired knowledge' is based on the substratum of 'Pure Knowledge' (Jñanarūpa

Ātman), which is eternally existent. Even if no new knowledge is acquired from outside, Pure Knowledge of Ātman exists all the time.

Ātman is Pure Consciousness that gets reflected in the mind (Antaḥkaraṇa). The Reflected Consciousness is called as Cidābhāsa (चिदाभास). It activates the mind and gives the mind the capacity to know, learn and understand new things. Because of the Reflected Consciousness, the mind starts thinking that it is sentient. The mind with the Reflected Consciousness knows the knowable objects with the help of the senses, and the knowing occurs on the substratum of Ātman. Knowable → Knowledge → Senses → Reflected Consciousness (Jīva) → Pure Consciousness (Ātman). If a seeker consistently ponders in this sequence, he may attain Aparokṣānubhūti of Brahman. Dṛk-Dṛśya Viveka also has intriguing explanation of Samādhi with the help of objects (Dṛśyanuviddha, दृश्यानुविद्ध) and Samādhi with the help of words (Shabdānuviddha, शब्दानुविद्ध). The Samādhi practiced with objects is directly related to the Śruti discussed here.

5. Specific experience: Consistent thinking with the help of scriptures and logic can first give a fair idea of the concept of Ātman as the Self, and then indeed lead one to the Self-realization.

Vedānta states that Brahman is (Pure) Existence, Consciousness, Bliss (Sat-Cit-Ānanda). Every being has innate experience of these three traits, as stated in the treatise of Advaita Makaranda -

अहमस्मि सदा भामि कदाचिन्नाहमप्रियः ।

*Ahamasmi sadā bhāmi kadacinnāhamapriyaḥ / (2)*

- I exist, I know my existence and I like myself.

Every being can instinctively experience these three facts about himself. The instinct 'I exist' derives from the Pure Existence, 'I know myself' derives from the Pure Knowledge and 'I like myself' derives from the Pure Bliss. These three basic instincts underscore the fact that 'I am Brahman, I am (Pure/Absolute) Existence, Consciousness and Bliss'. Brahman is the real nature of 'I'.

St. Jñāneśwara has written a verse that channelizes this thought process in the right direction -

देखे मनुष्यजात सकळ । हें स्वभावता भजनशीळ ।

जाहलें असे केवळ । माझ्याचि ठायीं ॥

*Dekhe manuśyajāta sakala / He swabhāvatā bhajanshīla /*

*Jāhale ase kevala / Mājhyāci ṭhāyī // (4.67)*

- All human beings are naturally My (Lord Kṛṣṇa's) devotees. They constantly sing My praises.

Lord Kṛṣṇa is (Pure) Existence, Consciousness, Bliss (Brahman, Sat-Cit-Ānanda). Every person has the natural instincts for survival, knowledge and happiness. Jīva receives these instincts from Brahman (Lord Kṛṣṇa). Jīva may not realize that he receives his innate instincts from Brahman, however they are reflected in his ardent desire to live, his quest for knowledge and his craving for happiness. The body is bound to die i.e. a person cannot live forever.

There is immense information in this world, and it is not possible to learn all the knowledge in one lifetime. The very nature of life is such that it is filled with both joyful and distressful incidents. So, it is not possible that the three instincts of survival, knowledge and happiness will get fulfilled using the worldly entities. However, Jīva can delve deep into the root of these three instincts and contemplate on Brahman as his real Self. Only then he will realize that the eternal Existence, Consciousness, Bliss (Sat-Cit-Ānanda) is his very nature. Eventually, he will not rely on his body to satisfy the instinct for survival. He will not rely on the vast worldly fields to satisfy his thirst for knowledge. He will not depend on the worldly objects for happiness. With consistent spiritual pursuit and guidance from Sadguru, Jīva can strive to attain Self-realization.

A seeker needs to nurture many qualities for Aparokṣānubhūti of Brahman. Detachment from worldly matters (Vairāgya, वैराग्य), discrimination between real and unreal (Viveka, विवेक), seeking the grace of Sadguru with faithful service, intense desire for liberation (Mokṣeccha, मोक्षेच्छा), being cognizant of the Vedāntic thought-process, maintaining forbearance (Titikṣa, तितिक्षा), and equipoise (Samādhāna, समाधान) in both favorable and adverse situations are some of the qualities required of a seeker. 'Who am I? What is the nature of this world? Who created this world? What is the purpose of human life?' are the quintessential questions faced by the human mind. A conscientious seeker should try to find out answers to these questions with the teachings of Sadguru and Upaniṣads. Humans are bound with three illusions –

- I am the body (DehaTadatmya Bhrānti),
- The world is real (JagatSatyatva Bhrānti)
- I am the doer-enjoyer of worldly matters (KartṛtvaBhoktṛtva Bhrānti).

The seeker should strive to liberate himself from the bindings of these illusions. He should carefully ponder on the difference between the worldly knowledge and the Pure Knowledge of Ātman. When a seeker learns, assimilates and applies the teachings of Vedānta in day-to-day life, he can realize Pure Bliss as his very nature. Only then, the teachings can be considered valuable in real sense.

Scriptural studies and spiritual practice both take a backseat, and Blissful life takes the center-stage after Self-realization. St. Jñāneśwara says that one should eventually detach from the notion of ingenuity and scholarliness in Vedānta and rejoice in the Pure Bliss of Brahman. He also expresses a sublime wish that more and more beings should benefit from Vedānta and lead a purposeful, rewarding life reveling in Pure Bliss of Brahman. Self-realization (Aparokṣānubhūti) of Brahman is the epitome of a glorious, elevated and triumphant human-life.

Dr. Shrikrishna Deshmukh
Murgud, Kolhapur

# Contents

# Aparokṣānubhūti

## Invocation verse

श्रीहरिं परमानन्दमुपदेष्टारमीश्वरम् ।
व्यापकं सर्वलोकानां कारणं तं नमाम्यहम् ॥ १ ॥

*Śri Hariṁ paramānandamupadeṣṭāramīśvaram /*
*Vyāpakaṁ sarva lokānāṁ Kāraṇaṁ taṁ namāmyaham // 1 //*

**Meaning:** I bow down to Śrihari, who is all-pervasive and the Supreme, Pure Bliss. He is Īśvara, the very first teacher and the cause of the Universe.

The word Śrihari stands for Īśvara, the ultimate governer. It may also indicate the One who imparts the greatest teaching. In India, it has been a sublime tradition to invoke the God with form (Saguṇa, सगुण) and without form (Nirguṇa, निर्गुण) at the beginning of each spiritual treatise. The word Paramānanda (परमानंद) indicates invocation of the formless God, while the word Namāmyaham (नमाम्यहम्) means bowing down to the God with form. The author Śri Śankara has shown an act of devotion towards both Saguṇa and Nirguṇa in this manner. It is not possible to worship formless Brahman. However, with the grace of Īśvara (Saguṇa Brahman), the treatise may be completed without any hurdles; hence, the author bows down to Īśvara. Śrihari (Nirguṇa Brahman) is omnipresent and all-pervasive. He is the cause of all plains (Lokas, लोक). Brahmasūtra states -

जन्माद्यस्य यतः ।

*Janmādyasya yataḥ / (1.1.2)*

- (Ātman is that) from which the origin, sustenance and dissolution of this (world derive).

Śrihari as Īśvara is the governer of the Universe and all activities take place under His system of governance. He is, thus, the supreme ruler (Bhagwāna, भगवान) of the world. The grace of Īśvara involves the grace of scriptures (Śāstrakṛpa, शास्त्रकृपा) and the author believes that the grace will ultimately lead this treatise to completion.

## The Fourfold boundaries (Anubandha Catuṣṭaya)

अपरोक्षानुभूतिर्वै प्रोच्यते मोक्षसिद्धये ।
सद्भिरेषा प्रयत्नेन वीक्षणीया मुहुर्मुहुः ॥ २ ॥

*Aparokṣānubhūtirvai procyate Mokṣasiddhaye /*
*Sadbhireṣa prayatnena vīkṣāṇīya muhurmuhuḥ // 2 //*

**Meaning:** This treatise of Aparokṣānubhūti is being presented to attain liberation (Mokṣa). Qualified seekers should strive to meditate upon the teaching (in this treatise) again and again.

It is an ancient Indian tradition that a Vedāntic treatise be composed within the purposeful limits of the Fourfold Boundaries (Anubandha Catuṣṭaya, अनुबंध चतुष्टय), which are-

1. **Qualified reader** - (*Adhikāri*, अधिकारी): Liberation (Mokṣa) is the only purpose of any treatise of Vedānta. The reader of this text should be an intense yearner of liberation.

   He should fulfill the Fourfold Prerequisites (Sādhana-Catuṣṭaya) for this purpose, which are -

- *Viveka* (विवेक) - Discrimination between the real and unreal aspets of life.
- *Vairāgya* (वैराग्य) - Dispassionate about the worldly objects and the other-worldly pleasures (heaven etc.)
- *Śamadishatak*, शमादिषटक (The set of six virtues) -
  - ➢ Control of the mind - Śama (शम)
  - ➢ Control of the organs - Dama (दम)
  - ➢ Renunciation - Uparama (उपरम)
  - ➢ Faith in scriptures, Īśvara, Sadguru - Śraddha (श्रद्धा)
  - ➢ Equipoise - Samādhāna (समाधान)
  - ➢ Forbearance - Titikṣā (तितिक्षा)
- *Mokśeccha* (मोक्षेच्छा) - Intense Desire for liberation

  These prerequisites will be studied in detail later in this text.

2. **Subject Matter** (*Viśaya*, विषय)**:** Self-realization (Knowledge of the Self as Ātman) is the main topic of this treatise. One should not wander in different directions other than the core topic.
3. **Relationship** (*Sambandha*, संबंध): This indicates relation between the reader and the treatise. A seeker who is desirous of Mokṣa is the main audience (Prayojya, प्रयोज्य) for this treatise, while the text itself is the

expounder (*Prayojak*, प्रयोजक). They have Prayoyojak-Prayojya relationship.

4. **Purpose** (*Prayojana*, प्रयोजन): This indicates the main benefit of studying the text. Reveling in the Pure Bliss as a result of the union of Jīva and Brahman (जीवब्रह्मैक्य) is the main benefit in this case.

The treatise written within the limits of these Fourfold Boundaries (*Anubandha*, अनुबंध) provides appropriate guidance to seekers. Ādi Śankara has explained these Anubandhas in the next eight shlokas.

## The Fourfold prerequisites (Sādhana- Catuṣṭaya)

स्ववर्णाश्रमधर्मेण तपसा हरितोषणात् ।
साधनं प्रभवेत्पुंसां वैराग्यादि चतुष्टयम् ॥ ३ ॥

*Swavarṇāśramadharmeṇa tapasā Haritoṣaṇāt |*
*Sādhanaṁ prabhāvetpuṁsāṁ vairāgyādi catuṣṭayam || 3 ||*

**Meaning:** Śrihari (God) is pleased with the execution of duties, which are prescribed as per the social order (*Varṇa*, वर्ण) and the stage in life (*Āśrama*, आश्रम). His graciousness helps the seeker in fulfilling the Fourfold Prerequisites.

In ancient times, Indian way of life was based on -

Social orders (*Varṇas*, वर्ण) -

- Brāhmin (ब्राह्मण) - Priestly class mainly responsible for teaching and religious activities
- Kṣatriya (क्षत्रिय) - Warrior class mainly responsible for ruling, security and administration

- Vaishya (वैश्य) - Business class mainly meant for production of goods and commercial progress
- Shudra (शूद्र) - Service class mainly meant for all kinds of assistance, cleaning, and laborious jobs

Stages in life (*Āśramas*, आश्रम)

- Brahmācāryaśrama (ब्रह्मचर्याश्रम) - Dedicating the body for serving to Śriguru, restraining from all forms of indulgence, and earning knowledge
- Grihasthaśrama (गृहस्थाश्रम) - Earning livelihood, taking care of family, performing religious rituals such as yajñās, donations etc.
- Vanapraṣṭhaśrama (वानप्रस्थाश्रम) - Going to seclusion such as a forest or a mountain, whole-heartedly pursuing spiritual studies.
- Sanyasaśrama (संन्यासाश्रम) - Officially renouncing the worldly life, leading ascetic life and dedicating the life for Self-realization.

The system of determining duties based on Varṇas and Āśramas is pretty much outdated in present times. One may argue whether the new change is good or bad, but the debate is not worth the time. Instead, we can embrace the reality and discuss what can be done practically in today's era and society. That the old system will resurrect and Īśvara will be pleased after fulfilling traditional duties, is just a distant daydream, which is of no use. St. Jñāneśwara has given a refreshing new perspective to the old system of social order and stages in life. He says -

**आणि मी माझें ऐसी आठवण । विसरले जयाचे अंत:करण ।**
**पार्था तो संन्यासी जाण । निरंतर ॥**

*Āṇi mi mājhe aisi āthavaṇa / Visarale jayāce Antahkaraṇa / Pārthā to sanyāsi jāṇa / Nirantara // (5.20)*

- An ascetic person or monk is the one who has forgotten the **I, me and mine** frame of mind.

He does not state the necesity to embrace official Sanyasaśrama here. He only asks us to forget the ego (I) and mineness pertaining to the body and individual self. When this distinctive awareness goes away, the seeker becomes a monk (Sanyasin) in essence.

It is possible to think about other Āśramas in the same manner. New-age definitions of the Āśramas would be -

- *Brahmācaryāśrama* (ब्रह्मचर्याश्रम) - Restrained behavior, being stronger and more confident, getting education
- *Grihasthāśrama* (गृहस्थाश्रम) - Working or doing business, earning livelihood, fulfilling duties towards one's immediate family, contributing in one's own capacity to society and nation
- *Vanaprasthāśrama* (वानप्रस्थाश्रम) - Formally retiring from the worldly and professional life, not interfering and giving unnecessary advice to others, seeking spiritual path without any external change in lifestyle (such as going in seclusion etc.),
- *Sanyasāśrama* (संन्यासाश्रम) - Renouncing 'I and my' mindset as prescribed by St. Jñāneśwara in the verse above.

One may continue worshipping Īśvara in the first three stages, while the fourth stage may be dedicated to studying for Self-realization. In this way, the main intent of the system of Āśramas can be fulfilled even in the new age.

St. Rāmadāsa says in Dāsabodha (*12.2.30*) that the society undergoes monumental change in the course of time. If a traditional, orthodox (Vedāntic) scholar doesn't change his approach with the changing times, who would care for his (conventional) wisdom or lifestyle? Who would benefit from his teaching or knowledge? He also expresses a revolutionary concept of being a Brahmin (priestly class) in his treatise Dāsabodha (*6.4.24*), which states that the Brahmin is the one, who has complete Knowledge of Brahman i.e. realized Brahman as his Self. [This idea is also stated in Upaniṣad.]

These thoughts are insightful and intriguing. Even today, there are many contradictory thoughts around the system of Varṇas and Āśramas. But who is willing to listen to those who can give authoritative answers? This itself is a question. Some traditional scholars still insist on following the Varṇa-Āśrama system. However, the society at large, is not inclined to follow these instructions.

Enlightened saints have explained many other non-traditional ways to propitiate Īśvara. We can easily embrace them even in the modern age. St. Jñāneśwara says-

**तया सर्वात्मका ईश्वरा । स्वकर्मकुसुमांची वीरा ।**
**पूजा केली होय अपारा । तोषालागीं ॥**

*Tayā Sarvātmaka Iśvarā / Svakarmakusumanchi virā /*
*Pūjā keli hoy apārā / Toshālāgi // (Jñā. 18.917)*

- When prescribed duties are done in a selfless manner, they (metaphorically) turn into beautiful flowers with pleasant smells. When we worship Īśvara by offering flowers of our own sublime actions, he is pleased.

In today's age, the word Swakarma (prescribed actions) does not just mean actions pertaining to one's Varṇa and Āśrama. One may define Swakarma as duties, which come one's way naturally, or which are accepted willfully in the new circumstances. The boundaries between Āśramas have faded over time. Today people from all Varṇas and castes perform actions beyond traditional duties prescribed by their birth or lineage. For example, many Brahmins (priestly class) are serving in Airforce, Navy or Army today. Many Marathas (warrior class) are in agriculture and production businesses.

Old people cannot retire to live secluded life in forests due to new-age responsibilities of grand-children, lack of forests, growing civilization, health issues, expensive medical treatment etc. It has become necessary to reconcile the definition of duties and responsibilities with new social transformations. Īśvara's grace can be earned with selfless, persistent execution of duties towards family and society. Worshipping Īśvara with utmost love, faith and knowledge of His real nature is also a great way to earn his pleasant grace. When Īśvara is pleased with actions and worship, His grace alone brings the seeker a genuine wish to earn the **Fourfold Means of Eligibility** (Sādhana-Catuṣṭaya) for spiritual pursuit. Ādi Śaṅkarācārya explains them in the next few verses.

## Detachment (Vairāgya)

ब्रह्मादिस्थावरान्तेषु वैराग्यं विषयेष्वनु ।
यथैव काकविष्ठायां वैराग्यं तद्धि निर्मलम् ॥ ४ ॥

*Brahmādisthāvarānteṣu vairāgyaṁ viṣayeṣvanu |*
*Yathaiva kākaviṣṭhayāṁ vairāgyaṁ taddhi nirmalam || 4 ||*

**Meaning:** One should feel completely disinterested in all pleasures offered by this world and the next world (heaven), just like the disgust one feels for the excreta of a crow. This is called as pure detachment (Nirmal Vairāgya, निर्मल वैराग्य).

The word Rāga (राग) means attachment. Virāga (विराग) means detachment and Vairāgya means the state of being detached from worldly pleasures. Muṇḍaka Upaniṣad (3.1.4) says that an enlightened person plays with his own Self (Ātmakrīḍa, आत्मक्रीड) and rejoices in the Pure Bliss of his own nature (Ātmarati, आत्मरती). The seeker who is strongly attached to the world (Dṛśyakrīḍa, दृश्यक्रीड) may never become Ātmakrīḍa. He cannot revel in the Pure Bliss of his own Self. Therefore, one should gradually detach from the worldly pleasures with careful discrimination between real and unreal (Viveka).

All objects that can be known by the five senses and the mind are termed as Dṛśya (दृश्य, perceived). Everything that is felt, remembered or understood is Dṛśya as well. Time, place, religion, language, thoughts, sentient and insentient beings, spirituality are part of Dṛśya. Some aspects of Dṛśya such as religion, scriptures, Vedānta, spiritual Master (Sadguru) are conducive, while others are deterrent for spiritual pursuit. A genuine seeker should limit his involvement in the world (Dṛśya) only to the matter related to earning livelihood. St. Jñāneśwara says that the Knowledge of Ātman cannot sustain and thrive without complete dispassion for the worldly matters (Jñā 15.36).

St. Sureśvarācārya says in Naiśkarmyasiddhi -

शुद्धमानं तु तच्चित्तमीश्वरार्पितकर्मभिः ।

वैराग्यं ब्रह्मलोकादौ व्यनक्त्यथ सुनिर्मलम् ॥

*Shuddhyamanan tu taccittamīśvararpitakarmabhih /*

*Vairāgyam Brahmalokādau vyanaktyatha sunirmalam // (1.47)*

- One who surrenders to Īśvara and offers results of all actions to Him, gradually attains pure mind and develops complete dispassion for all worldly and heavenly pleasures.

The quest for the ultimate Supreme, Pure Knowledge of Ātman awakens only in the pure mind.

St. Sureśvarācārya further says -

व्युत्थिताऽशेषकामेभ्यो यदा धीरवतिष्ठते ।

तदैव प्रत्यगात्मानं स्वयमेवाऽविविक्षति ॥

*Vyutthita'sheshkamebhyo yada dhiravatiṣṭhate /*

*Tadaiva pratyagamatmanam swayameva Vivikṣati // (1.48)*

- Ātman is pure and uncontaminated. One who develops complete dispassion for all worldly desires, and remains calm, unperturbed under all situations, feels natural, instinctive need for Self-realization.

Detachment or dispassion (Vairāgya) can be developed in three stages -

- *Guṇakārya* (गुणकार्य) *Vairāgya* - dispassion for the gross world (people, objects, events, circumstances)
- *Guṇamaya* (गुणमय) *Vairāgya* - dispassion for the subtle world (activities of the mind, intellect, memory, ego)
- *Guṇagandha* (गुणगंध) *Vairāgya* - dispassion even from the thought that 'I am dispassionate'

The seeker gradually feels dispassionate about all sense pleasures as he evolves through these three stages.

## Discrimination between real and unreal (Viveka)

नित्यमात्मस्वरूपं हि दृश्यं तद्विपरीतगम् ।
एवं यो निश्चयः सम्यग्विवेको वस्तुनः स वै ॥ ५ ॥

*Nityamātmaswarūpaṁ hi dṛśyaṁ tadviparītagam /*
*Evaṁ yo niścayaḥ samyagviveko vastunaḥ sa vai //5 //*

**Meaning:** Ātman is real and eternal, while the world (Dṛśya, दृश्य) is unreal and transient. This discrimination (between real and unreal) and conviction about Ātman are called as Viveka.

Viveka is one of the foremost qualifications of a seeker. Ādi Śaṅkarā has stated the gist of Vedānta in one sentence-

ब्रह्मसत्यं जगन्मिथ्या ।

*Brahma-Satyaṁ Jaganmithyā /*

- Brahman alone is real; the world is unreal.

Discrimination between real and unreal (Satya-Mithyā), eternal and transient (Nitya-Anitya), sentient and insentient (Jaḍa-Cetana), core and peripheral (Sāra-Asāra) are various forms of Viveka, but they are ultimately the same. For example, the material objects are peripheral (Asāra, असार) and they give only finite, transient (Anitya, अनित्य) happiness. Also, one needs to work very hard, face many obstacles and deal with uncertainties while trying to obtain the worldly objects. Comparison, jealousy, conflict and the duality of joy-grief are inevitable while striving to earn worldly pleasures (Viśaya, विषय) in life. St. Tukārāma says that one gets money, luxuries, good-will and respect only as per his Prārabdha (destiny). Fame, wealth, success and prosperity make a person happy. However, Vedānta says that this happiness is not experienced due to any external worldly object, or fame, wealth etc. The mind (Antaḥkaraṇa) becomes completely quiet as a result of fulfillment of a desire (e.g. being fmaous). The mind disappears in Ātman, its very own Self momentarily, when it acquires the objects of desire. St. Jñāneśwara says that the worldly happiness is only a result of this fleeting union of Jīva with Brahman when a desire is fulfilled (Jñā. 13.131).

Objects give only transient happiness; therefore, one should not work towards accumulating them in life. The worldly life should gradually take a backseat. The seeker should contemplate on the eternal, Pure Bliss of Ātman, which is his own nature. This thoughtful discrimination and conviction about the eternal nature of Ātman lead to Self-realization. The treatises written by Ādi Śaṅkarācārya such as AnātmaŚrivigarhanam (अनात्मश्रीविगर्हणम्) and Ātmabodha (आत्मबोध) explain the nature of Viveka in detail.

## Control of the mind (Śama), control of organs (Dama)

**सदैव वासनात्यागः शमोऽयमिति शब्दितः ।**

**निग्रहो बाह्यवृत्तीनां दम इत्यभिधीयते ॥ ६ ॥**

*Sadaiva vāsanā tyāga Śamo'yamiti śabditaḥ |*

*Nigraho bāhyavṛttīnām Dama ityabhidhīyate || 6 ||*

**Meaning:** The word Śama (शम) indicates constant renunciation of all Vāsanās in the mind, while Dama (दम) indicates constant restraint of outgoing organs.

Vāsanās (वासना) are the subtle imprints in the mind, which result from pending desires of the past births. St. Tukārāma says that one needs to completely eradicate all Vāsanās in the mind and restrain organs from going outwards, in order to turn them in towards Ātman.

Vāsanās are of four kinds -

- Desire about the body (*Dehavāsanā*, देहवासना) - Firm belief that 'I am body' causes one to develop strong affinity in the body. This affinity leads to the desire to live as long as possible, which is called as Dehavāsanā.
- Desire for objects (*Viśayavāsanā*, विषयवासना) - Most people associate happiness with material objects. This leads to the desire to acquire many objects and enjoy them without hurdles, which is called as Viśayavāsanā.

- Desire for appreciation (*Lokavāsanā*, लोकवासना) - The desire for constant appreciation and recognition from others is called as Lokavāsanā. It results in the need to be surrounded only by people who shower praise all the time. Desire for enjoying pleasures in other worlds (Lokās) such as heaven, is called Lokavāsanā as well.
- Desire for learning scriptures (*Śāstravāsanā*, शास्त्रवासना) - When one gets deep insight into Vedānta, it sometimes creates a strong craving for learning as many scriptures as possible and being an erudite scholar. Comparison and jealousy enter consequently in the mind.

The seeker should renounce these desires gradually as guided by the scriptures. For that, he should strive to control organs, which constantly flow outvards in the world to acquire and enjoy objects. St. Kabira gives a valuable guidance in this regard. He says -

**मन गया तो जाने दे । मत जाने दे शरीर ।**

**नही खिची कमान तो । कहांसे छूटेगा तीर ॥**

*Mana gayā to jāne de / Mata jāne de sarira /*

*Nahi khinchi kamān to / Kahānse chutegā tira //*

- An arrow cannot be thrown from the bow so long as one doesn't pull the string. Similarly, the mind may crave for many objects, but the organs cannot go out to the world when they are leashed under strict control.

This means, even if one is unable to practice Śama (control of the mind), he should resolutely practice Dama (control of the organs). When organs are reined in, mind is compelled to follow the organs. Both Śama and Dama are thus interdependent and connected with each other.

Vāsanās reside in the intellect (Buddhi, बुद्धि). The intellect takes decisions (to enjoy sense pleasures) according to a Vāsanā and conveys the decision via mind to organs. Organs then actually execute actions to acquire objects and enjoy them. Katha-Upaniṣad has beautifully explained this concept using the metaphor of a chariot (1.3.3). One should understand the chain of Vāsanā-intellect-mind-organs-objects of enjoyment, and how they all work together. The chain clearly demonstrates that eradication of Vāsanās (dormant desires) from the mind (Śama, शम) is imperative for Self-realization.

Wishes and desires are born in the mind (Manas, मन). Decisions (to fulfill a desire) are made in the intellect. Citta firmly holds on to the decision made by the intellect. When a Vāsanā is dominant, most decisions are made to fulfill an incomplete Vāsanā. However, if the new inputs of Vedānta are taken in by organs, they are conveyed by the mind to the intellect and imprinted in the intellect. For some time during spiritual practice, there is an intense conflict in the intellect between old imprints of Vāsanā and new imprints of Vedānta.

Consistent listening to discourses, reading of scriptures, following the guidance of Sadguru and deep contemplation of Vedānta strengthens the new imprints in the intellect. Old imprints of Vāsanās are gradually eradicated and replaced by new imprints of Vedānta. The intellect then decides to retract from sense pleasures and pursue the spiritual path. Citta learns to hold on to the new decisions made by the intellect. Eventually, the mind, the intellect and the Citta work in complete harmony to progress on the spiritual path. This is an incredible result of consistent listening to the discourses and contemplating on Vedānta. Both Śama and Dama can be practiced in this manner.

## Renunciation (Uparati) and Fortitude (Titikṣā)

विषयेभ्यः परावृत्तिः परमोपरतिर्हि सा ।
सहनं सर्वदुःखानां तितिक्षा सा शुभा मता ॥ ७ ॥

*Viṣayebhyaḥ parāvṛttiḥ paramoparatirhi sā /*
*Sahanam sarvaduḥkhānām titikṣā sā śubhā matā // 7 //*

**Meaning:** Complete renunciation of all sense pleasures is called as Uparati (उपरती). Patient fortitude to deal with pain and sorrow of all kinds without the slightest complaint is called as Titikṣā (तितिक्षा).

Uparati is achieved when Śama and Dama are practiced in entirety. In Śama and Dama there is a conscious practice to restrain the mind and organs. However, Uparama means natural, effortless restraint that results in complete dispassion of the worldly pleasures.

Life is full of the duality of joy-grief and many other conflicts. If one continues to nurture joy and grief, it would be impossible to tread the path of Self-realization. It is difficult to travel from distressful life to the Pure Bliss of Ātman (travel is a word used only for conceptual convenience here). Even the worldly joy needs to be kept aside on the path of Self-realization, so surely there is no place for grievous thoughts in this journey. Titikṣā involves facing all obstacles in the journey patiently and enduring all griefs and afflictions without any complaint. However, Titikṣā certainly does not mean inflicting unnecessary torture on body under the name of spiritual practice. E.g. extreme form of fasting, following harsh rituals, walking bare-foot for long distance etc. should be avoided.

## Faith (Śraddha), Concentration (Samādhāna)

निगमाचार्यवाक्येषु भक्तिः श्रद्धेति विश्रुता ।

चित्तैकाग्र्यं तु सल्लक्ष्ये समाधानमिति स्मृतम् ॥ ८ ॥

*Nigamācārya vākyeṣu bhaktiḥ śraddheti viśrutā |*

*Cittaikāgryam tu sallakṣye samādhānamiti smṛtam || 8 ||*

**Meaning:** Utmost faith in the teachings of the Vedas and Sadguru is called as Śraddha (श्रद्धा). Deep concentration of the mind on only One principle of Brahman is called as Samādhāna (समाधान).

Nurturing utmost faith in the doctrine of Vedānta and teachings of Sadguru is highly important and imperative for spiritual pursuit. Lord Kṛṣṇa says in Bhagvad-Gītā -

श्रद्धावान्लभते ज्ञानं तत्परः संयतेन्द्रियः ।

*Śraddhāvān labhate jñānam tatparaḥ samyatendriyaḥ | (4.39)*

- One realizes Pure Knowledge (of Ātman) only with utmost faith, promptness of spiritual practice and the control of organs.

However, only faith is of no use. Praśnopaniṣad mentions a tale of six disciples, who surrender to Sadguru and request Him to guide them. Sadguru, in turn, asks them to practice faith, austerities (Tapas, तप) and restraint on sensual desires (Brahmācārya, ब्रह्मचर्य) for one year. This indicates that every seeker of Mokṣa needs to practice austerities and restraint of sensual desires in addition to nurturing faith in the teachings of Vedānta. The word संयतेन्द्रियः (Sanyatendriyaḥ) in Gītā indicates similar practice. Faith in the teachings of Sadguru and scriptures eradicates the two types of incorrect beliefs (Doṣa, दोष) from the mind.

- **Asambhāvanā Doṣa** (असंभावना दोष) - The erroneous thought that 'the principle named Ātman cannot possibly exist', is called as Asambhāvanā Doṣa. Ātman cannot be seen, touched, heard, smelt or felt with the senses. This gives rise to various doubts in the mind such as, 'Ātman cannot possibly exist, or I cannot possibly be Ātman'. These skeptical thoughts constitute the Asambhāvanā Doṣa.
- **Viparīta Bhāvanā Doṣa** (विपरीत भावना दोष) - Incorrect ideas such as 'Mind is Ātman, intellect is Ātman, Prāṇa is Ātman, Śūnya is Ātman, I am body, and the visible world is real', are called as Viparīta Bhāvanā Doṣa.

These and all other doubts, confusions and questions about Ātman should be addressed systematically and clarified for spiritual pursuit.

One-pointed concentration on the principle of Ātman is called as Samādhāna. It is imperative to establish it Self-realization. Various factors such as Rajoguṇa, skepticism, and illusions like 'I am body' or 'the world is real' create many distractions in the mind. Distracted mind cannot concentrate on the One Ātman. Therefore, it is necessary to eliminate all distractions in the mind.

## Desire for liberation (Mumukṣātva)

संसारबन्धनिर्मुक्तिः कथं स्यान्मे दयानिधे ।
इति या सुदृढा बुद्धिर्वक्तव्या सा मुमुक्षुता ॥ ९ ॥

*Saṁsārabandhanirmuktiḥ kathaṁ syānme dayānidhe /*
*Iti yā sudṛdha buddhirvaktavyā sā mumukṣutā // 9 //*

**Meaning:** One who intensely pines for liberation from the bondages of the world is called as Mumukṣu (मुमुक्षु).

There are three kinds of people who yearn for liberation. They are -

- Weak desirer - It is good to get Mokṣa.
- Medium desirer - I should get Mokṣa.
- Intense desirer - I want only Mokṣa and nothing else.

Constant deep pondering on the doctrine of Vedānta and detachment from sense pleasures can lead a seeker from being a weak to an intense desirer of liberation. St. Tukārāma says that accumulation of pure pious virtues (Shuddha Puṇya, शुद्ध पुण्य) of many past births leads to the strong desire of liberation. This indicates absolute necessity for a seeker to work in a selfless manner in order to accumulate pure virtues (merits) in life. It also indicates the necessity to nurture Sattvaguṇa. St Samartha Rāmadās Swāmi says that Sattvaguṇa leads to love and devotion to the God while Rajoguṇa leads to the cycle of birth-death. Without the accumulation of pure virtues, the curiosity and desire for Mokṣa does not awaken or intensify in the mind.

## Guidance for the seeker

उक्तसाधनयुक्तेन विचारः पुरुषेण हि ।
कर्तव्यो ज्ञानसिद्ध्यर्थमात्मनः शुभमिच्छता ॥ १० ॥

*Uktasādhanayuktena vicāraḥ Puruśena hi /*
*Kartavyo jñānasiddhyarthamātmanaḥ śubhamiccata // 10 //*

**Meaning:** One who desires perpetual welfare in life, should acquire the **Fourfold Means of Eligibility** (Sādhana-Catuṣṭaya) as mentioned in the previous verses, contemplate on the Knowledge of Ātman and the fact that Ātman is his very nature.

Ādi Śaṅkarācārya says in his text Viveka Cūdāmaṇi -

वस्तुसिद्धिर्विचारेण न किंचित् कर्मकोटिभिः ।

*Vastusiddhīrvicāreṇa na kiñcit-karma-koṭibhiḥ /*

- Vastu means the principle of Brahman. **I am Brahman** can be realized only with deep contemplation and not with millions of activities.

The union of Jīva and Brahman can be achieved only with constant thinking and contemplating on Brahman. Vedānta treatises and texts authored by saints point to the same fact that pondering or contemplation is the best spiritual practice. All saints themselves are profound thinkers. Contemplation done with selfless action and worship is highly effective for Self-realization. All saints encourage selfless action and worship with equal emphasis. They also propel us to detach from worldly matters. Consistent thinking with the help of Vedāntic scriptures, treatises written by saints, and the teachings of Sadguru escort us smoothly towards liberation.

## Emphasis on knowledge

नोत्पद्यते विना ज्ञानं विचारेणान्यसाधनैः ।
यथा पदार्थभानं हि प्रकाशेन विना क्वचित् ॥ ११ ॥

*Notpadyate vinā jñānaṁ vicāreṇānyasādhaṇāiḥ* /
*Yathā padārtha bhānaṁ hi prakāśena vinā kvacit* // 11 //

**Meaning:** It is not possible to think about Ātman (discriminate between real and unreal) without the knowledge of scriptures, just as an object cannot be seen (with mere eyes) without the light.

St. Jñāneśwara explains the characteristics of ignorance (Ajñāna) by stating that one who does not study the Upaniṣads, dislikes the theory of Yoga and cannot immerse himself in the study of spiritual scriptures is ignorant in nature. This means that the one who studies these three texts, knows Ātman, becomes One with Ātman and his ignorance is eradicated.

Ignorant people live under three kinds of illusions -

- 'The world is real' illusion (Jagat-satyatva Bhrānti, जगत्सत्यत्त्व भ्रांति)
- Identification of the Self with the body (Deha-tādātmya, देहातादात्म्य)
- 'I am the doer' illusion (KartṛtvaBhoktṛtva Bhrānti, कर्तृत्वभोक्तृत्व भ्रांति)

A seeker should work arduously to eradicate these illusions with the help of Guruvākya **Tat Tvam Asi** *(You are that,* तत्त्वमसि), which is the main teaching of a Sadguru. The seeker should strive to purify his mind and immerse it in Ātman. He should carefully study the basics of Vedānta and clarify the core concepts such as sentience-insentience, illuminor-illumined and Adhiṣṭhāna-Adhyāsta etc. Consistent study of Vedānta ultimately leads him to Mokṣa.

## Primal Analysis

**कोऽहं कथमिदं जातं को वा कर्तास्य विद्यते ।**
**उपादानं किमस्तीह विचारः सोऽयमीदृशः ॥ १२ ॥**
*Ko'haṁ kathamidaṁ jātaṁ ko vā kartāsya vidyate |*
*Upādānaṁ kimastīha vicāraḥ so'yamīdṛśaḥ || 12 ||*

**Meaning:** Who am I? How is this world created? Who is its creator? What is the 'material cause' of this world? This is a method of philosophical analysis.

These questions have been addressed in detail in Upaniṣads, Bhagvad-Gītā, Brahmasūtras and subsequent related texts authored by luminary scholars and saints. Texts and treatises written by enlightened saints analyze intricate details of these questions. Ātman (Pure Consciousness, the real Self) cannot be realized with any action. Selfless actions purify the mind and enable it to disappear in Ātman, which is only One, eternal principle. Consciousness cannot be created or produced by action. There are many misconceptions about the real Self such as 'I am body, I am mind, I am rich or poor, I am short or tall, I am fat or thin' etc. They are related to identification with the gross and the subtle body. The real Self largely remains unknown due to ignorance.

The origin of the world has been explained with the help of the Higgs Boson theory or the God Particle by modern Science. In Vedānta, the world is considered as an illusive appearance (Mithyā). However, since most people believe the world to be real, Vedānta presents two types of theories about the creation of the world. One theory states that the world was created instantaneously (Yugapat, युगपत्). The other theory of false-attribution (Adhyāropa) states that the world was created sequentially step-by-step. However, since the world is illusive in nature, the theory of its creation should not be given much importance either way.

## Who am I?

नाहं भूतगणो देहो नाहं चाक्षगणस्तथा ।

एतद्विलक्षणः कश्चिद्विचारः सोऽयमीदृशः ॥ १३ ॥

*Nāhaṁ bhūtagaṇo deho nāhaṁ chākṣāgaṇastatha /*

*Etadvilakṣaṇaḥ kascidvicāraḥ so'yamīdṛśaḥ // 13 //*

**Meaning:** I am neither the body created from the five great elements, nor am I the five senses. I am different from them. This is a method of philosophical analysis.

St. Rāmadāsa says that the body is just a collection of various elements. But all elements are 'mine', so they cannot be 'me'. For example, house is 'mine', so 'I' am not the house, 'I' am clearly different from the house. Similarly

- Body is 'mine', so I am different from the body. 'I' am not the body.
- I apply 'my' mind to the work. My mind is clearly an instrument used in the execution of the work. So, my mind is not 'me'. 'I' am not the mind.
- I regulate 'my' Prāṇa in Prāṇayama. Prāṇa are mine, so 'I' am not Prāṇa.

These examples prove the fact that my existence is not dependent on the existence of Prāṇa. Ādi Śaṅkarācārya has given a long list of elements in his famous hymn NirvanaShatakam (निर्वाणषटक), where he says that I am neither the mind, nor intellect, nor memory, nor Ego. I am (Pure) Existence, Consciousness, Bliss (Sat-Cit-Ānanda, सत्-चित्-आनंद).

## Another way of philosophical analysis

अज्ञानप्रभवं सर्वं ज्ञानेन प्रविलीयते ।

सङ्कल्पो विविधः कर्ता विचारः सोऽयमीदृशः ॥ १४ ॥

*Ajñānaprabhāvaṁ sarvaṁ jñānena pravilīyate /*

*Saṅkalpo vividhāḥ kartā vicāraḥ so'yamīdṛśaḥ // 14 //*

**Meaning:** This entire universe (Dṛśya, दृश्य) is created from ignorance and it becomes inconsequential (for all practical purposes) after attainment of the Knowledge of Brahman. Actions are performed for fulfillment of desires, and the doer is created for performing actions. This is a method of philosophical analysis.

'Who created the universe? How is it created? When and why was it created?' These are quintessential questions. Many scholars have presented theories that attempt to answer these questions, however, these theories can always be refuted with systematic analytical thinking.

Some theorists claim that Īśvara (the God) is the creator of this Universe, however, they cannot deterministically show His presence. One theory claims that the Universe is just a recreational game of the God (Līla, लीला), however this thought does not seem logical anyway. What kind of game is it, where Jīva is mandated to go through the cycle of birth and death, and further asked to liberate himself by following arduous systems of actions, worship and knowledge (Karma, Upāsanā and Jñāna)?

One theory claims that the Universe is created from subtle subatomic particles (Paramanu, परमाणु), however, the particles are insentient. So how can sentient entities be created from insentient particles? Some theorists (Mimansakas, मीमांसक) claim that the world is created from actions, but who is the doer of these actions? Is he sentient or insentient? If one strives to search for the original creator by going back in time, it may lead to infinite chain

(Anavasthā Doṣa, अनवस्था दोष) that ultimately leads to nothing. There are other theorists who advocate Śūnya, Pradhāna or Kṣanika Vijñāna as the cause of this universe. However, these theories are very fuzzy and incomplete (Brahmasūtra Śānkarbhāṣya). Hence, only an enlightened person, who knows the cause of the universe, can explain the creation of the universe in a definite manner. His explanation can answer all questions and put all doubts to rest. One can see the eternal Truth only in the light of the Pure Knowledge of Brahman.

Vedānta states that the universe is only an appearance based on various desires and imaginations in the mind. For the one who controls the mind (desires), the world is sublated and it does not appear as real. St. Rāmadāsa says in Dāsabodha -

मुळी सर्पाकार देखिली । येक भ्याला येके वोळखिली ।

*Muli sarpākār dekhilī / yeka bhyālā yeke volakhilī / (9.3.40)*

- In a dim light, a snake is delusively seen instead of a branch of a tree. Some recognize it to be a branch, while some get scared assuming it to be a real snake.

Similarly, the world falsely appears on the substratum of Brahman. Some people recognize it as Brahman, while some think that the world is real and get tormented by it.

St. Sureśvarācārya says -

अस्तु वा परिणामोऽस्य दृशेः कूटस्थरूपतः ।

कल्पितोऽपि मृषैवासो दण्डस्येवाप्सु वक्रता ॥

*Astu va parinamo'sya dṛsheh kutastharupah /*

*Kalipto'pi mṛshaivaso dandsyevapsu vakrata // (Nai. Si. 2.84)*

- A wooden stick immersed in water is appears to be bent at an angle, even when it is straight and partially immersed in water. Similarly, the diversified universe is but an appearance, and only One Brahman is the reality. Many other verses in Upanisads and scriptures state the same fact.

## Example of philosophical analysis

एतयोर्यदुपादानमेकं सूक्ष्मं सदव्ययम् ।
यथैव मृद्घटादीनां विचारः सोऽयमीदृशः ॥ १५ ॥

*Etayorupadānamekaṁ sūkṣmaṁ sadavyayam /*
*Yathaiva mṛdghatādīnāṁ vicāraḥ so'yamīdṛśaḥ // 15 //*

**Meaning:** The clay is the 'material cause' of all pots. Similarly, these two (ignorance, अज्ञान and desire, संकल्प) are the 'material cause' of the universe. Only One, eternal, subtle and transcendental principle (Brahman) exists in reality. This is a method of philosophical analysis.

Pots may come in various sizes, shapes and colors, however, only the clay is the 'material cause' (Upādāna Kāraṇa, उपादान कारण) and a potter is the 'instrumental cause' (Nimitta Kāraṇa, निमित्त कारण) of all pots. A potter is different from pots, while the clay is included in pots. The clay has a form and it can be made wet with water.

Brahman is formless, and it cannot be made wet with water. So, Brahman cannot be considered as just the 'material cause' of the universe. Brahman is the only One, eternal principle, hence it cannot be just the 'instrumental cause' of the Universe like potter. Brahman is AbhinnaNimittopādānaKāraṇa (अभिन्ननिमित्तोपादानकारण), which means that the 'material cause' and 'instrumental cause' of the world is one and the same.

Brahmasūtra says-

जन्माद्यस्य यतः ।

*Janmādyasya yataḥ / (1.1.2)*

- (Ātman is that) from which the origin, sustenance and dissolution of this (world derive).

The world is but an illusion, which appears real due to ignorance, desires, thoughts or imaginations (Saṅkalpa, संकल्प). This is called as the theory of 'false attribution' (Adhyāropa). The existence of the world cannot be substantiated in any other way. This entire thought process is a systematic analytical enquiry in Vedānta.

## I denoted by Ātman is Brahman

अहमेकोऽपि सूक्ष्मश्च ज्ञाता साक्षी सदव्ययः ।

तदहं नात्र सन्देहो विचारः सोऽयमीदृशः ॥ १६ ॥

*Ahameko'pi sūkṣmaśca jnātā sākṣi sadavyayaḥ /*

*Tadahaṁ nātra sandeho vicāraḥ so'yamīdṛśaḥ // 16 //*

**Meaning:** Ātman, which is denoted by the word 'I', is the only One, the knower, the Witness, all-pervasive, eternal, subtle, and unchanging principle. There is no doubt that Ātman is Brahman and I am that Brahman. This is a method of philosophical analysis.

Brahman is the substratum of the universe. So long as the universe is considered as real, its creation and existence are attributed to ignorance and desires (Saṅkalpa, संकल्प) in the mind, as per the theory of Adhyāropa. Brahman is sentient, while the world is insentient and 'falsely cognized' (Adhyāsta, अध्यस्त) on Brahman. All humans are part of the world and their bodies are insentient in nature. Insentient entities do not have the capacity to know, learn or understand anything. The insentient body is wrongly perceived as sentient due to the presence of Reflected Consciousness (Cidābhāsa, चिदाभास) in it. Cidābhāsa is just a reflection of Pure Consciousness (Ātman). Brahman is the substratum (Adhiśthāna, अधिष्ठान) while body is Adhyāsta on Brahman. Therefore, Ātman (Pure Consciousness limited to a body) and Brahman (Pure Consciousness that pervades everywhere) are one and the same.

Ātman is not the knower. Every Jīva has a mind with Cidābhāsa, which gains knowledge of objects on the substratum of Ātman, hence Jīva is the knower. Ātman is Absolute Knowledge (Jñānarūpa) or the ultimate Knower.

There is a verse in Bṛihadāraṇyaka Upaniṣad:

**न हि द्रष्टुर्दृष्टेः विपरिलोपो भवति ।**

*Na hi draṣṭurdṛuṣṭeḥ viparilopo bhāvati / (4.3.23)*

- The vision of the Knower never ceases, since the Knower is imperishable. There is nothing separate from the Knower that it could know.

Acquiring knowledge of objects involves the triad of knower, knowable and knowing. The knowledge with the triad is termed as Qualified Knowledge (Vṛttijñāna, वृत्तिज्ञान). However, Ātman is Cit (Pure Knowledge), which is not dependent on the triad. Ātman is the ultimate Knower that cannot be known by anything or anyone. Ātman never ceases to be Absolute, Pure Knowledge through the states of waking, dream and deep-sleep. In the state of deep-sleep, there is no Qualified Knowledge, however, the eternal, Pure Knowledge of Ātman is still present. In this context, Ātman is called as the ultimate Knower, Perceiver or Seer (Jñātā-ज्ञाता, Mantā-मन्ता or Draṣṭā-द्रष्टा).

When a desire or thought (Saṅkalpa, संकल्प) arises in the mind, it is due to ignorance (of the real Self). St. Jñāneśwara says that Jīva realizes he is Brahman when thoughts and desires in his mind disappear completely (Jñā. 6.82). A seeker who is contemplative and meditative in nature can enquire in this manner about his real Self.

## Ātman is organless, body has multiple organs

आत्मा विनिष्कलो ह्येको देहो बहुभिरावृतः ।
तयोरैक्यं प्रपश्यन्ति किमज्ञानमतः परम् ॥ १७ ॥

*Ātmā viniṣkalo hyeko deho bahubhirāvṛtaḥ /*
*Tayoraikyaṁ prapaśyanti kimajñānamataḥ param // 17 //*

**Meaning:** Ātman is undivided and without parts, so it is only One, while a body is made up of many organs. Even then, they (body and Ātman) are considered as one, what else can be bigger ignorance than this?

In ignorance, Jīva invariably identifies himself with the body. The feeling that 'I am body' completely pervades the human life. In reality, Ātman is the only One without division or separation of any kind. It transcends the three dimensions of past, present and future. It is present equally, everywhere, and at all times. The formless, attributeless Pure Consciousness is the real nature of the Self. The body, on the other hand, consists of many millions of cells and different organs. Humans have eternally identified their real Self with the body (form and organs). This is the biggest ignorance. This ignorance can be eradicated only with the Pure Knowledge of the Self (Ātman). Those, who are attached to the worldly life cannot gain the Knowledge of Ātman and attain Self-realization.

## Ātman is internal, body is external

**आत्मा नियामकश्चान्तर्देहो बाह्यो नियम्यकः ।**

**तयोरैक्यं प्रपश्यन्ति किमज्ञानमतः परम् ॥ १८ ॥**

*Ātmā niyāmakascāntardeho bāhyo niyamyakaḥ /*

*Tayoraikyaṁ prapaśyanti kimajñānamataḥ param // 18 //*

**Meaning:** Ātman resides in the body, governs the body from within yet remains detached from it. The body is external to Ātman and gets regulated by Ātman. Even then, these two (body and Ātman) are considered as one, what else can be bigger ignorance than this?

Upaniṣad states the same face in this verse -

**असंगोऽह्ययं पुरुषः ।**

*Asaṅgo'hyayam Puruṣaḥ / (Bru. Up. 4.3.15)*

- This Puruṣa (Brahman) is Unattached.

Ātman pervades all sentient, insentient entities, yet remains completely detached from them. For example, the space is present inside all pots, yet the space is detached from them. A pot and its internal space are completely different. It is incorrect to consider them to be one and the same. Similarly, it is incorrect to consider the Self (Pure Consciousness or Ātman) and body as one with each other. Ignorant people consider the body as the Self. This ignorance is beginingless. It has continued just like a stream of water since the very beginning of the world. In a water-current, droplets keep changing, yet the stream remains the same. Similarly, the beginningless stream of ignorance continues for all ignorant people. It comes to an end only for the one who attains the Knowledge of the Self. Ātman governs the body by being the substratum for Vāsanās. Vāsanās impel each Jīva to perform actions due to which Jīva gets caught in the cycle of birth and death.

## **Ātman is pure & illuminor, body is impure, illumined**

**आत्मा ज्ञानमयः पुण्यो देहो मांसमयोऽशुचिः ।**
**तयोरैक्यं प्रपश्यन्ति किमज्ञानमतः परम् ॥ १९ ॥**
*Ātmā jñānamayaḥ puṇyo deho māṁsamayo'suciḥ /*
*Tayoraikyaṁ prapaśyanti kimajñānamataḥ param // 19 //*

**आत्मा प्रकाशकः स्वच्छो देहस्तामस उच्यते ।**
**तयोरैक्यं प्रपश्यन्ति किमज्ञानमतः परम् ॥ २० ॥**
*Ātmā prakāśaka svaccho, dehastāmasa ucyate /*
*Tayoraikyaṁ prapaśyanti kimajñānamataḥ param // 20 //*

**Meaning:** Ātman is the pure, Absolute Knowledge. The body is perishable flesh and impure. Even then, they (body and Ātman) are considered as one, what else can be bigger ignorance than this? (19)

Ātman is clean, spotless and the illuminor (Prakāśaka, प्रकाशक), while the body is the result of darkness of ignorance (Tamoguṇa, तमोगुण). Even then, they (body and Ātman) are considered as one, what else can be bigger ignorance than this? (20)

Vedānta states that the world appears to be real only due to ignorance (Tamoguṇa). All bodies are created from Tamoguṇa. Pure Consciousness (Ātman) is Self-effulgent and pure. All bodies are known only in the divine light of Pure Consciousness. One insentient entity cannot know the other insentient entity. One stone cannot gain the knowledge of another stone. Similarly, one body cannot know the other body just by itself. Each body has sentient Jīva with Reflected Consciousness (Cidābhāsa) in it. Each Jīva gains knowledge of his own body and other bodies using the five senses in the light of Self-effulgent Ātman. How can we possibly measure the depth of ignorance of a person, who doesn't understand this reality?

## Ātman is eternal, body is transient

आत्मा नित्यो हि सद्रूपो देहोऽनित्यो ह्यसन्मयः ।
तयोरैक्यं प्रपश्यन्ति किमज्ञानमतः परम् ॥ २१ ॥

*Ātmā nityo hi sadrūpo deho'nityo hyasanmayaḥ |*
*Tayoraikyaṁ prapaśyanti kimajñānamataḥ param || 21 ||*

**Meaning:** Ātman is eternal and Pure Existence that transcends the three times, while the body is transient and exists for a limited time. Even then, they (body and Ātman) are considered as one, what else can be bigger ignorance than this?

The word Sat (सत्) denotes the eternal Truth or Satya (सत्य). It means Pure Existence, which exists in the three times of past, present and future. Sat (Ātman) transcends time. The body does not exist before birth and after death. Ātman is beginingless, birthless, ageless and endless, thus eternal and ever-available (Nitya, नित्य) in nature.

Body goes thorugh the changes of being infant, toddler, adult, old etc. Everyday, Jīva experiences the three states of being awake, dream and deep-sleep. Jiva feels the duality of joy and grief. Jīva has three Guṇas - Sattva, Rajas and Tamas. However, Ātman is changeless, stateless, non-dual and attributeless (Nirguṇa, निर्गुण) in nature. Thus, Ātman and body are entirely different from each other. What can we possibly say to those ignorant people, who consider them to be one?

## Self-effulgent Ātman

**आत्मनस्तत्प्रकाशत्वं यत्पदार्थावभासनम् ।**
**नाग्न्यादिदीप्तिवद्दीप्तिर्भवत्यान्ध्यं यतो निशि ॥ २२ ॥**

*Ātmanastatprakāśatvaṁ yatpadārthāvabhāsanam |*

*Nāgnyādidīptivaddīptirbhāvatyāndhyaṁ yato niśi || 22 ||*

**Meaning:** The sun, the moon and the fire have their own (physical) light. However, their light undergoes changes. Ātman is Self-effulgent, and the light of Ātman is not subject to any change.

The luminosity and light of the sun are of the kind of fire. One should carefully discern the difference between the light of the sun and the light of Ātman. One can 'see' in the light of the sun, however, one can 'know what is seen' only in the light of Ātman. There is a root word in Sanskrit named Div (दिव्) from which two other words have been formed, named Divā and Deva. The word Divā (दिवा, lamp) indicates (physical) light in which one can 'see' things. The word Deva (देव) stands for the subtle, divine light in which one can 'know' the seen things. St. Jñāneśwara says that the divine light is the one that illumines intellect of all beings.

The sunlight can grow brighter or be dimmer. It shines differently in different parts of the world. The moon is known for its changing size throughout the month. The light of the fire changes as per the fuel fed to it. However, the light of Ātman is changeless. It is ever-shining and ever-available in the same quantity, everywhere, at all times. It does not change with the changing states of Jīva. Atharvashirsha (an Upaniṣadic hymn for praising Lord Ganeśa) has described Brahman in this manner -

त्वं गुणत्रयातीतः । त्वं देहत्रयातीतः । त्वं कालत्रयातीतः ।

*Tvam guṇatrayatitah / Tvam dehatrayatitaha /*

*Tvam kalatrayatitah /*

- Oh Lord Ganeśa! You are above and beyond the three Guṇas (Sattva, Rajas, Tamas), the three bodies (gross, subtle, causal) and the three times (past, present, future).

Brahman is present everywhere (Sarvatra, सर्वत्र). There is no place where it is not present. It is also called as Vibhu (all-pervasive). It is present at all times (Sadā, सदा). Vedānta states that it is beginning-less, perpetual and the eternal Truth (Anādi, Nitya, Satya - अनादि, नित्य, सत्य). It is present in the same quantity (Sama, सम) everywhere. The goal of spiritual pursuit is to realize that this all-pervasive Brahman is our real Self.

## Spiritually ignorant person

देहोऽहमित्ययं मूढो मत्वा तिष्ठत्यहो जनः ।
ममायमित्यपि ज्ञात्वा घटद्रष्टेव सर्वदा ॥ २३ ॥

*Deho'hamityayaṁ mūḍho matvā tiṣṭatyaho janaḥ /*
*Mamāyamityapi jñātva ghatadraṣṭeva sarvadā // 23 //*

**Meaning:** A person who owns a pot knows that 'the pot is mine, so it is evidently separate from me. I am not the pot'. On the contrary, when the same person sees his own body, he thinks that 'I am the body'. In reality, the body belongs to him (therefore he is separate from the body). This, verily, is the ignorance.

The thought that 'I am body' is a manifestation of human ignorance. Delusional mind is the result of ignorance, while eradication of the delusion is the nature of the Knowledge. Ātman, the real Self, is covered by the limiting adjunct (Upādhi, उपाधी) of the body. So, the body is mistakenly considered as the real Self (I). This process is called as 'mutual superimposition' (Anyonyadhyāsa, अन्योन्याध्यास). Ātman is real, while the body is unreal (transient). However, the body is considered real and Ātman is considered unreal. Ignorant person thinks 'I am the body and I will die some day'. However, every person is essentially Ātman, which is eternal, birthless and endless.

## Brahman is Sat-Cit-Ānanda

**ब्रह्मैवाहं समः शान्तः सच्चिदानन्दलक्षणः ।**
**नाहं देहो ह्यसद्रूपो ज्ञानमित्युच्यते बुधैः ॥ २४ ॥**

*Brahmaivāhaṁ samaḥ śāntaḥ saccidānandalakṣāṇaḥ /*
*Nāhaṁ deho hyasadrūpo jñānamityucyate budhaiḥ // 24 //*

**Meaning:** I am Brahman. I am peace. I pervade everywhere equally. I am (Pure) Existence, Consciousness, Bliss (Sat-Cit-Ānanda). I am not the body, which is bound to die. This careful reflection is called as the real Knowledge by the wise.

Sama (सम): Sama means equal. Brahman pervades equally in this diverse universe, which has divisions of many kinds such as the three Guṇas (Sattva, Rajas, Tamas), millions of species, the three states (waking, dreaming, deep-sleep), various plains (earth, heaven), and various types of God etc. Despite all these differences in the universe, Brahman itself is monolithic. It is not divided or separated in any way.

Śānta (शान्त): Śānta means peace. Brahman does not ever loose its eternal peace, despite of major or minor events in the world. The Jīva may feel excited, perturbed, happy, jealous, hopeful or dejected, but Ātman is never disturbed in any way. Māṇḍūkya Śruti says -

एकात्मप्रत्ययसारं प्रपञ्चोपशमं शान्तं शिवमद्वैतम् ।

*Ekātmāpratyayasaram Prapañcopashamam*

*Shantam Shivamadvaitam | (1.7)*

- (Ātman is) without division, auspicious, non-dual, and the only One, where the entire Universe ceases to exist. It is also described as 'peace' in this same verse.

Sat-Cit-Ānanda: Pure Consciousness (Ātman) is also named as Sat-Cit-Ānanda Brahman.

- Sat denotes eternal, Absolute, Pure **Existence** that negates non-existence or transient existence of objects known to Jīva.
- Cit denotes eternal, Pure **Consciousness**, which negates the limited knowledge or ignorance experienced by Jīva.
- Ānanda denotes eternal, Pure **Bliss**, which negates the constant duality of joy-grief experienced by Jīva.

One should first gain the Parokṣa Jñāna (theoretical knowledge) that 'I am Brahman'. When one gains the direct, first-hand realization that 'I am not the body, I am Brahman', it is called as Aparokṣa Jñāna (अपरोक्ष ज्ञान).

- I am Sat, so I am neither born, nor will I die.
- I am Cit, so I am not touched by ignorance in any way.

- I am Ānanda, so I do not experience grief of any kind.
- I am Pure Consciousness, which is ever-liberated. However, I appear to be bound in a limited body-mind system as a Jīva. I am Ātman, which is never limited or bounded by body, space and time.

This is the Knowledge of the Self as conceded by the wise.

## Brahman is changeless, formless

निर्विकारो निराकारो निरवद्योऽहमव्ययः ।
नाहं देहो ह्यसद्रूपो ज्ञानमित्युच्यते बुधैः ॥ २५ ॥

*Nirvikāro nirākāro niravadyo'hamavyayaḥ /*
*Nāhaṁ deho hyasadrūpo jñānamityucyate budhaiḥ // 25 //*

**Meaning:** I am changeless (Nirvikāra), formless (Nirākāra), unaffected by afflictions (Niravadya) and do not undergo decay of any kind (Avyaya). I am not the body that is bound to perish. This careful reflection is called as the real Knowledge by the wise.

Nirvikāra (निर्विकार): Vikāra means change. The body undergoes six changes -

- Birth (Jāyate - जायते)
- Existence (Asti - अस्ति)
- Growth (Vardhate - वर्धते)
- Change (Vipariṇamate - विपरिणमते)
- Decay (Apakṣīyate - अपक्षीयते)
- Death (Mriyate - म्रियते)

However, 'I am not the body'. I am formless, organless Ātman, so I do not undergo any change. I am changeless (Nirvikāra, निर्विकार).

<u>Nirākāra</u> (निराकार): Ākāra means form. Different particles of atoms come together so a 'form' can be seen. However, Pure Consciousness (Ātman) is Niravayava (निरवयव), which means it is not made up of particles. It has no shape, no form and no organs.

<u>Niravadya</u> (निरवद्य): The three inflictions Ādhaytmika Tāpa, Ādhibhoutika Tāpa and Ādhidaivika Tāpa are imposed on the body, or the mind.

Results of an action are desired by the mind, and it is the mind that gets upset when actual results do not match the expected results. These inflictions, miseries and griefs do not ever affect the real 'I' i.e. formless Ātman. The mind may be affected by fear, but Ātman is beyond fear of any kind as stated in the Śruti –

**द्वितीयाद्वै भयं भवति ।**

*Dvitīyādvai bhayaṁ bhāvati / (Bṛ. Up. 1.4.2)*

- Where there is a second, there is fear.

<u>Avyaya</u> (अव्यय): Vyaya (व्यय) means decay. Pure Consciousness does not have decay of any kind, since it pervades everywhere, in the same amount and at all times.

The wise concede that I am this Pure Consciousness (Ātman) and not the perishable body.

## Brahman is free from diseases, all-pervading

निरामयो निराभासो निर्विकल्पोऽहमाततः ।
नाहं देहो ह्यसद्रूपो ज्ञानमित्युच्यते बुधैः ॥ २६ ॥

*Nirāmayo nirābhāso nirvikalpo'hamātataḥ /*
*Nāhaṁ deho hyasadrūpo jñānamityucyate budhaiḥ // 26 //*

**Meaning:** I am free from all diseases and changes (Nirāmaya). Nobody can comprehend me using routine methods of gaining knowledge (Nirābhāsa). I am beyond options, doubts, ideas and even imaginations of all kinds (Nirvikalpa) and omnipresent, vast, expansive (Atatah). I am not the body that is bound to die. This careful reflection is called as the real Knowledge by the wise.

Nirāmaya (निरामय): Āmaya (आमय) means disease. The body (gross, subtle, karana) is inflicted with many diseases (physical, mental, intellectual), since it has a form and many organs. However, I am Pure Consciousness, which is formless and organless. So, I do not ever suffer from any disease.

Nirābhāsa (निराभास): Ābhasa (आभास) means knowledge. Nirābhāsa means one that cannot be known or learnt. Ātman is Self-cognizant. Being formless, it cannot be comprehended by routine means (Pramāṇa) of gaining knowledge such as perception, presumption, inference (प्रत्यक्ष, अर्थापत्ती, अनुमान) etc. The knowledge gained using the five senses or the mind is called as Vṛttijñāna (वृत्तिज्ञान, Qualified knowledge). However, Ātman is beyond the senses. Knowing Ātman is a direct process. The seeker can only know Ātman by being One with it. The triad of knower, knowable, and knowing disappears when one knows Ātman to be his Self.

Nirvikalpa (निर्विकल्प): Vikalpa means option. To choose an option, at least two entities are necessary. However, Pure Consciousness is only One, non-dual and without divisions of any kind. Hence it is Nirvikalpa (निर्विकल्प).

Śruti describes Ātman as -

**ओतश्च प्रोतश्च ।**

*Otaśca protaśca /*

- (One which is present) inside and outside of every object (without any space in between).

Ātata (आतत): Ātman is boundless. It completely pervades everything in this universe and beyond. The body exists in limited space and time. It is bound to die, so it cannot be the all-pervasive, eternal Absolute Ātman.

I am Ātman and not the perishable body. This is the knowledge of the real Self as conceded by the wise.

## Brahman is attributeless

**निर्गुणो निष्क्रियो नित्यो नित्यमुक्तोऽहमच्युतः ।**
**नाहं देहो ह्यसद्रूपो ज्ञानमित्युच्यते बुधैः ॥ २७ ॥**

*Nirguṇo niṣkriyo nityo nityamukto'hamacyutaḥ /*
*Nāhaṁ deho hyasadrūpo jñānamityucyate budhaiḥ // 27 //*

**Meaning:** I am Attributeless (Nirguṇa), actionless (Niṣkriya), eternal (Nitya), ever-liberated (Nityamukta) and one that cannot degrade (Acyuta). I am not the body that is bound to perish. This careful reflection is called as the real Knowledge by the wise.

Nirguṇa (निर्गुण): I am Ātman, which is beyond the three attributes (Guṇas) of Sattva, Rajas, Tamas. I am Nirguṇa (निर्गुण). So, the manifestations of Guṇas such as being pure, greedy or lazy do not apply to me.

Īśvara (Brahman+Māyā) has six Guṇas -

1. Success (Yasha, यश) - Every desire (Saṅkalpa) of Īśvara has success. The universe is created and destroyed just by His desire. Every desire of Īśvara is fulfilled.
2. Wealth (Śri, श्री) – Īśvara is the original owner, governer of the entire wealth in the world (money, estate, elements of nature, prosperity, fortune and the spiritual wealth of Mokṣa etc.)
3. Benevolence (Audārya, औदार्य) – Īśvara is the most benevolent of all. He owns the five great elements, all planets and everything else in the world. But He Himself is formless. He gives organs (sense and action) to Jīva so Jīva can enjoy the worldly matter. Later, He gives Himself to the devotee who, surrenders into Īśvara unconditionally.
4. Detachment (Vairāgya, वैराग्य) – Īśvara is the creator and governor of the world, and pervades the world completely yet remains detached from it.
5. Royalty (Aiśvarya, ऐश्वर्य) – Īśvara has the power to regulate the world (Ishatā, ईशता). He regulates all sentient and insentient beings. E.g. the sun rises and sets in a pattern, ocean does not cross its boundaries,

every year has four seasons etc. The world operates as per the system of governance created by Īśvara.

6. Knowledge (Jñāna, ज्ञान) – Īśvara has the knowledge of His real Self as Brahman all the time. He pervades the world, so He is the Knower and Witness of everything (Sarvajñā-सर्वज्ञ, Sarvasakṣi-सर्वसाक्षी). He is the only one with complete knowledge.

However, Brahman does not have these six Guṇas hence known as Nirguṇa (निर्गुण).

Niṣkriya (निष्क्रिय): Kriyā (क्रिया) means action. Ātman does not have a form, so it cannot execute any action. It does not have the sense organs or the actions organs as stated by Muṇḍaka Upaniṣad (1.1.6). Jīva is the doer, while Ātman is non-doer.

Nitya (नित्य): Nitya (नित्य) means eternal. Pure Consciousness is ever-existent. It exists everywhere, equally, at all times (Sarvatra, Sadā, Sama). An object can be non-existent in one of the four ways:

1. Prior non-existence (Prāgabhāva, प्राक् अभाव) - Non-existence of an object before creation.
2. Posterior non-existence (Pradhvamsābhāva, प्रध्वंस अभाव) - Non-existence following destruction.
3. Absolute non-existence (Atyantābhāva, अत्यंत अभाव) - Absolute non-existence in all times. E.g. horns of a hare.
4. Mutual non-existence (Anyonyābhāva, अन्योन्य अभाव) - Absence of one entity in the other and vice-versa. E.g. a flower is absent in a chair and vice versa.

Ātman (Dṛk) cannot be non-existent in any way.

Nitya-Mukta (नित्यमुक्त): Mukta (मुक्त) means 'liberated'. Pure Consciousness is ever-liberated. It is beyond the concept of bondage and liberation. The concept of liberation (Mokṣa) is applicable only so long as one is bounded by the thoughts that 'I am the body'.

Acyuta (अच्युत): Cyuta (च्युत) means 'falling down' or 'perishing' or 'degrading'. Pure Consciousness pervades everywhere, so it cannot fall down to another place. It is formless i.e. it does not have a body. So, it is indestructible and imperishable. It cannot be burnt, cut or made wet as explained in Bhagvad-Gītā (2.24). It remains the same just the way it is.

The wise concede that I am Pure Consciousness (Ātman) and not the perishable body.

## Brahman is pure, immovable

**निर्मलो निश्चलोऽनन्तः शुद्धोऽहमजरोऽमरः ।**

**नाहं देहो ह्यसद्रूपो ज्ञानमित्युच्यते बुधैः ॥ २८ ॥**

*Nirmalo niścalo'nantaḥ śuddho'hamajaro'maraḥ |*

*Nāhaṁ deho hyasadrūpo jñānamityucyate budhaiḥ || 28 ||*

**Meaning:** Ātman is completely clean (Nirmala), immovable (Nishchala), endless (Ananta), pure (Shuddha), ageless (Ajara) and deathless (Amara).

**Nirmala** (निर्मल): Pure Consciousness (Ātman) is clear and clean. It is not contaminated with the three states (waking, dreaming and deep-sleep); the three Guṇas (Sattva, Rajas, Tamas) and the three bodies (gross, subtle, causal). It is formless, so it cannot have these or any other impurities, which are normally found in Jīva with the body.

**Niśchala** (निश्चल): Ātman pervades everywhere, so it is immovable. It cannot be moved to another place since there is no place where all-pervasive Ātman is not present.

**Ananta** (अनन्त): Ātman is beginingless, hence it is endless as well. It is eternal and transcends time.

**Śuddha** (शुद्ध): Jīva has a mind, which is full of impurities such as lust, greed, anger etc. However, Ātman does not have these impurities, hence it is pure (Śuddha, शुद्ध).

**Aja** (अज), **Ajara** (अजर) and **Amara** (अमर): Ātman does not have a body or a form. Hence it is birthless (Aja-अज), ageless (Ajara-अजर) and deathless (Amara-अमर).

This is a nature of real Knowledge of the Self as conceded by the wise.

## Refuting the theory of Śūnyavāda

स्वदेहं शोभनं त्यक्त्वा पुरुषाख्यञ्च सम्मतम् ।
किं मूर्ख शून्यमात्मानं देहातीतं करोषि भोः ॥ २९ ॥

*Svadehaṁ śobhanaṁ tyaktvā Puruṣākhyañca sammatam /*
*Kiṁ mūrkha śūnyamātmānaṁ dehātītaṁ karoṣi bhoḥ // 29 //*

**Meaning:** O ignorant one! It has been established that Ātman pervades the body completely yet remains detached from it. Why do you assert this Ātman to be non-existent?

Śūnya means absolute nothingness. Pure Consciousness cannot be non-existent (Śūnya). Any real or imaginary entity cannot be created from that, which is non-existent. Ātman is eternal, Pure Existence that is the very substratum of the universe. All entities exist on substratum of Ātman.

Those who support the theory of Śūnya may insist that 'nothing' can be Ātman. For example, in the process of meditation, the seeker may gradually leave behind (disconnect from) his gross body, subtle body etc. and arrive at a point where he thinks 'nothing' is his real self (Ātman). If we keep thinking that the body is not Ātman, the mind is not Ātman etc., eventually no entity will exist for which we might say 'this is not Ātman'. Existence of no entity means Śūnya or absolute non-existence. In meditation, one may reach the state of nothingness (Śūnya) and experience immence peace in that stage. The entire world (joy, sorrow, excitement, fear, misery, worry etc.) is refuted and discarded at this stage in meditation. Some might mistake this non-existence of the world (Śūnya) as Brahman. However, this is an indication of dumb thinking according to St. Rāmadāsa. He says -

इकडे दृश्य तिकडे देव । मध्ये शून्यत्वाचा ठाव ।
तया प्राणी मंदबुद्धिस्तव । ब्रह्म म्हणे ॥

*Ikaḍe dṛśya tikaḍe deva / Madhye śūnyatvācā thāva /*
*Taya prāṇi mandabuddhistava / Brahma mhaṇe // (Dās. 8.10.66)*

- On one side there is Brahman or the God, on the other side there is the visible world. In between, there is nothingness (Śūnya, शून्य). Senseless, foolish people call it as Brahman.

One can know that 'this is Śūnya or nothingness' only in the ever-available light of Ātman. Ātman is called as MahaŚūnya of Śūnya (supreme nothingness) in the same context.

The light of Ātman illumines the pure intellect and enables it to know everything. All actions in the universe take place in the light of Ātman. All kinds of knowledge pertaining to memory, logic, illusion, ignorance, scriptures etc. are acquired on the substratum of Ātman. The lives of all beings are replete with knowledge. In such case, why be foolish by calling the substratum Ātman as non-existent?

## Ātman is separate from the body

स्वात्मानं शृणु मूर्ख त्वं श्रुत्या युक्त्या च पूरुषम् ।
देहातीतं सदाकारं सुदुर्दर्शं भवादृशाम् ॥ ३० ॥

*Swatmānaṁ śṛnu mūrkha tvam śṛtyā yuktyā ca Pūruṣam /*
*Dehātītaṁ sadākāram sudurdarsaṁ bhāvādṛśām // 30 //*

**Meaning:** O ignorant one! Decide with the help of logical reasoning and Upaniṣads that Ātman is separate from the body. Ātman is eternal, Pure Existence (Sat, सत्) that transcends time. It is always cognized in the form of existence. It is very difficult for (ignorant) people like you to realize this knowledge.

Katha Upaniṣad says -

अस्ति इति उपलब्धव्यो ।

*Asti iti upalabdhavyo | (2.3.13)*

- In millions of names-forms, it (Ātman) exists in the form of 'existence'. [Existence is the very nature of Sat.]

Chāndogya Upaniṣad says –

सत् एव सोम्य इदमग्र आसीत् ।

*Sat eva somya idamagra Āsit | (6.2.1)*

- Only Sat (Pure Existence) existed before the beginning of this universe.

Sat transcends past, present and future. It exists irrespective of any object or person in the world. From Sat, the concept of Asti (अस्ति, existence) and many other names-forms came into existence. All objects, people, events and circumstances exist on the substratum of Sat. It may be easy to understand the existence with respect to people or objects. However, it is extremely difficult to comprehend the concept of intrinsic existence that is not dependent on any person, object or perceivable entity. People, who are extrovert, outgoing, ignorant and materialistic, find it very hard to understand this theory of Absolute, Pure Existence. Without sharp, pure and subtle intellect, it is not possible to see the principle of Sat, which is the very substratum of existence of all objects.

## Ātman is One, bodies are many

अहंशब्देन विख्यात एक एव स्थितः परः ।
स्थूलस्त्वनेकतां प्राप्तः कथं स्याद्देहकः पुमान् ॥ ३१ ॥

*Ahaṁśabdena vikhyāta eka eva sthitaḥ paraḥ /*
*Sthūlastvanekatāṁ prāptaḥ kathaṁ syāddehakaḥ pumān // 31 //*

**Meaning:** Ātman denoted by 'I' is the Supreme (principle) and only One, whereas gross bodies are many. So how can Ātman be the same as the body?

In the treatise named Advaita Makaranda, Kavi Laxmidhara says -

अहमस्मि सदा भामि कदाचिन्नाहमप्रियः ।

*Ahamasmi sadā bhāmi kadācinnāhamapriyaḥ / (2)*

- I exist, I know my existence and I like myself.

Every person can instinctively experience these three facts about himself. 'I exist, and I know myself' – these words denote the fact that every being is always aware of the existence of 'I'.

St. Jñāneśwara says -

एऱ्हवीं सर्वांच्या हृदयदेशीं । मी अमुका आहें ऐसी ।
जे बुद्धि स्फुरे अहर्निशीं । ते वस्तु गा मी ॥

*Erhavi sarvāñcyā hṛdayadeśī / Mi amukā āhe aisī /*
*Je buddhi sphure aharnisī / Te vastu gā mī // (Jñā. 15.421)*

- 'I am this' or 'I am that' kind of awareness is present constantly in the mind of one and all. I am verily that constant awareness about the Self i.e. Ātman.

There are two types of ego (Ahaṅkāra) -

- **Superimposed ego** (Adhyāsta, अध्यस्त) - 'I am great', 'I am beautiful', 'I am ugly', 'I am rich' are examples of superimposition of the ego on the body and circumstances.
- **Substratum ego** (Adhiṣṭhāna, अधिष्ठान) - The constant instinct of existence 'I am' is the substratum ego (Ātman / Sat).

Eradication of superimposed ego (अध्यस्त अहं) is of utmost importance in spiritual pursuit. In Soham meditation, the superimposed ego contemplates that 'I am Saha or Brahman'. Once superimposed ego is eradicated, one can realize the substratum ego (अधिष्ठान अहं), which has constant, eternal existence (Sat).

Ego (Ahaṅkāra, अहंकार) is insentient since it is made up of the earth (Pṛthvi, पृथ्वी) element. But when ego is combined with Reflected Consciousness (Cidābhāsa, चिदाभास), there is an illusion of sentience in it, due to which superimposed 'I' is wrongly considered as sentient.

In everyday life, (superimposed) ego has many manifestations such as, 'I am tall' (body), 'I am foolish' (intellect), 'I am rich' (circumstance), 'I am famous' (society), 'I am devotee' (God), 'I am loving' (as father, mother, son, daughter etc.), 'I am a leader' (power), 'I am successful' (job), 'I am a father' (family), 'I am an owner' (house) etc. The basic, general ego pertaining to day-to-day activities, is not troublesome for spiritual pursuit in any way. However, when conceit, vanity and attitude enter in the ego, it creates duality, divisions in the mind and disrupts the spiritual pursuit. Hence, Bhaktiyoga (the path of devotion) states the dictum that 'everything belongs to the God', while Jñānayoga and Vedānta propound that 'the worldly life is a result of destiny (Prārabdha, प्रारब्ध) and one acquires it as per the scheme of Īśvara'. St. Tukārāma says in his devotional poetry that one receives wealth, money, prestige, respect etc. only according to his Prārabdha. These thoughts clearly indicate that the generic, common, all-pervasive 'I' (Ātman) is very different from the specific, limited, bounded 'I', which is manifested in day-to-day life. How can this universal, One, Supreme Ātman be limited to many body-mind systems or many names-forms?

## Jīva is the perceiver, body is perceived

अहं द्रष्टतया सिद्धो देहो दृश्यतया स्थितः ।

ममायमिति निर्देशात्कथं स्याद्देहकः पुमान् ॥ ३२ ॥

*Ahaṁ draṣṭrutayā siddho deho dṛsyatayā sthitaḥ /*

*Mamāyamiti nirdeśātkathaṁ syāddehakaḥ pumān // 32 //*

**Meaning:** In the statement, 'this (body) is mine', Jīva (I) is clearly the perceiver (Draṣṭā, द्रष्टा) while body is the perceived (Dṛśya, दृश्य). So how can Ātman be the same as the body?

We generally address the body as 'my body'. It is common to feel that 'my body is aching'. Nobody ever says, 'I am aching'. Thus, it is evident that 'I' am separate from 'my body'. Jīva is the perceiver (subject), while the body is the perceived (object). In this case, the perceiver is very closely glued to the perceived, so they are incorrectly assumed to be one and the same.

## Ātman is constant, body is subject to changes

अहं विकारहीनस्तु देहो नित्यं विकारवान् ।
इति प्रतीयते साक्षात्कथं स्याद्देहकः पुमान् ॥ ३३ ॥

*Ahaṁ vikārahīnastu deho nityaṁ vikāravan /*
*Iti pratiyate sakṣāt kathaṁ syāddehakaḥ pumān // 33 //*

**Meaning:** Ātman does not undergo any change, while the body is constantly subject to change. So, how can Ātman be the same as the body?

Bhagvad-Gītā describes Ātman as -

अजो नित्यः शाश्वतोऽयम् पुराणो ।

*Ajo nityaḥ śāśvatao'yam purāṇo / (2.20)*

- (This Ātman is) birthless, eternal, and the most primeval.

Bhagvad-Gītā describes the body as -

अन्तवन्त इमे देहा ।

*Antavanta ime deha / (2.18)*

- These bodies are bound to end.

देहिनोऽस्मिन्यथा देहे कौमारं यौवनं जरा ।

*Dehino'sminyathā dehe koumāraṁ youvanaṁ jarā / (2.13)*

- The body undergoes the stages of being infant, young and old.

These stages of body are based on the six changes (Vikāras) [See verse 25]. How can the body and Ātman be the same when they are poles apart from each other?

As a body, I am subject to many changes; however, as Ātman I am changeless. One can clearly learn that 'I am chageless Ātman, so I will not grow old or die'. Constant thinking in this manner leads to peaceful and fearless life.

## Ātman is the eternal Truth, body is perishable

यस्मात्परमिति श्रुत्या तया पुरुषलक्षणम् ।
विनिर्णीतं विशुद्धेन कथं स्याद्देहकः पुमान् ॥ ३४ ॥

*Yasmātparamiti śṛtyā tayā Puruṣalakṣānam /*
*Vinīrnitam viśuddhena kathaṁ syāddehakaḥ pumān // 34 //*

**Meaning**: Wise men (Ṛṣi) describe Puruṣa (Ātman) as the Highest Truth. So how can Ātman be same as the (inferior) body?

It is said that eternal (superior) Ātman lives in and through the perishable (inferior) body in a detached manner. How can the perishable be the same as the eternal? Ātman is present where the body is present, however, the body is not neecssarily present where Ātman is present. In other words, there is Anvaya (अन्वय, presence) of Ātman inside body, however, there is Vyatireka (व्यतिरेक, absence) of body in Ātman. The text of Advaita Makaranda presents a unique approach in this regard -

नच स्वजन्मनाशं वा द्रष्टुमर्हति कश्चन ।
तौ हि प्रागुत्तराभावचरम प्रथम क्षणौ ॥

*Na ca swajanmanāśam vā draṣṭumarhati kaścan /*
*Tou hi prāguttarabhāvacaram prathama kṣānou // (15)*

- Nobody can experience his own birth and his own death. It is not possible to ever experience the moment just before birth and the moment just after death.

An object can be non-existent in one of the four ways [see Verse 27]. The word Prāgabhāva (प्राक् अभाव) stands for prior non-existence i.e. non-existence of an object before creation. Each Jīva had Prāgabhāva before its birth. The moment this Abhāva (non-existence) comes to an end, Jīva takes a birth. Even the most intellectual, brilliant person cannot experience the moment before his birth. If Jīva has no existence before birth, how can he possibly experience his own birth? After death, there is non-existence of Jīva, so how can he experience it? Therefore, if Jīva cannot experience his own birth and death, how can Ātman, which is birthless and deathless, be experienced? In such case, how can they be one and the same?

## Ātman is all-pervading, body is pervaded

सर्वं पुरुष एवेति सूक्ते पुरुषसंज्ञिते ।
अप्युच्यते यतः श्रुत्या कथं स्याद्देहकः पुमान् ॥ ३५ ॥

*Sarvaṁ Puruṣa eveti sūkte Puruṣasandnite /*
*Apyucyate yataḥ śṛtyā kathaṁ syāddehakaḥ pumān // 35 //*

**Meaning:** Puruṣasūkta (Śruti, a verse in Veda) says that all of this (world) verily is Puruṣa, and He is all that was in the past and that will be in the future. So how can Ātman be the same as the body?

The text mentioned in this verse is a part of Ṛgveda (10.90.2). Many other verses in Vedas, Bhagvad-Gītā and Upaniṣads point to the fact that 'everything is Brahman'.

- रसो वै सः ।

  *Raso vai saḥ / (Tai. Up. 2.7)*

- Brahman is the essence of the entire creation. It is Bliss.

- नेह नानास्ति किञ्चन ।

  *Neha nānāsti kiñcan / (Katha. Up. 2.1.11)*

- Other than Brahman, nothing else exists.

- एकमेवाद्वितीय ।

  *Ekamevādvitiya / (Chān. Up. 6.2.1)*

- Brahman is verily the only One, without a second.

- वासुदेवः सर्वमिति ।

  *Vāsudevaḥ saravamiti / (Gītā. 7.19)*

- One should uninterruptedly reflect that everything is essentially Vāsudeva (Lord Kṛṣṇa i.e. Brahman).

- एकधातुर्द्रष्टव्यं ।

  *Ekadhāturdraṣṭavyam / (Chān. Up. 6.2.1)*

- Brahman has no differences, distinctions (Bheda, भेद) of any of the following three kinds –

  - Self-difference (*Swagata Bheda*, स्वगत भेद) – Difference within a single object. E.g. within a fruit of apple, we find seeds, skin, pulp, stalk etc.
  - Intra-difference (*Swajātīya Bheda*, स्वजातीय भेद) – Difference between two objects of the same species.

E.g. apple and kiwi are both fruits, but different from each other.

- <u>Inter-difference</u> (*Vijatīya Bheda*, विजातीय भेद) - Difference between two objects of different species. Apple is different from trees, stones etc.

No such differences exist in Brahman.

When all scriptures point to this fact, how can one imagine the existence of body seperately and assert that Ātman (I) is the same as the body?

## Ātman is detached, body is attached to impurities

**असङ्गः पुरुषः प्रोक्तो बृहदारण्यकेऽपि च ।**
**अनन्तमलसंसृष्टः कथं स्याद्देहकः पुमान् ॥ ३६ ॥**

*Asaṅgaḥ Puruṣaḥ prokto Bṛhadāraṇyake'pi ca /*
*Anantamalasaṁsṛṣṭaḥ kathaṁ syāddehakaḥ pumān // 36 //*

**Meaning:** Bṛhadāraṇyaka Upaniṣad also says that this Puruṣa is detached (*Asaṅga*, असंग). The body is, however, attached to many impurities. So how can Ātman be same as the body?

Every person is attached to many impurities including his own body. Jīva lives in the company of his friends, relatives (sentient); home, vehicle (insentient); enmity, love, jealousy (emotions), germs (inside and outside body); dreams, memories etc. These are not considered as impurities in routine life, and there is no reason to do so. In spiritual pursuit, they are called as impurities only when one gets attached to them. Attachment involves everything from love, hatred, jealousy, fear etc. From the Vedāntic perspective, they are all illusive in nature. Poet St. Laxmidhara explains this concept using a beautiful example in his treatise Advaita Makaranda -

अमृताब्धेर्न मे जीर्णिर्मृषाण्डिण्डीर जन्मभिः ।
स्फटिकार्द्रेर्न मे रागः स्वाप्नसंध्याभ्रविभ्रमैः ॥

*Amṛtābdherna me jirṇirmrushāṇdiṇdīra janmabhiḥ /*
*Sphatikārdrena me rāgaḥ svāpnasandhyābhravibhramaiḥ //*

- White clouds linger in the sky in the evening. Imagine a very tall mountain made up of clear crystals standing in front of those clouds. When sun-rays peep out of the clouds, their seven colors pervade the crystal mountain and create beautiful scenic display. But even if the mountain looks colorful, it is not actually colored. Colors are just reflected in it.

Similarly, there are no bodies or objects in Brahman. Body and Brahman (I) can never be one, just as sun-rays and crystal mountain are never one with each other.

## Ātman is illuminor, body is illumined

तत्रैव च समाख्यातः स्वयंज्योतिर्हि पूरुषः ।
जडः परप्रकाश्योऽयं कथं स्याद्देहकः पुमान् ॥ ३७ ॥

*Tatraiva ca samakhyātaḥ swayañjyotirhi Pūruṣaḥ /*
*Jaḍaḥ paraprakāśyo'yam kathaṁ syāddehakaḥ pumān // 37 //*

**Meaning:** In the same manner, Puruṣa is described as Self-effulgent. Puruṣa is sentient and illuminor, while body is insentient, and it gets illumined by Puruṣa. So how can Ātman be the same as the body?

Bṛhadāraṇyaka Upaniṣad says -

अत्रायम् पुरुषः स्वयं ज्योतिः ।

*Atrāyam Puruṣaḥ swayañjyotih / (4.3.9)*

- This Ātman is Self-effulgent

Ātman is Pure Knowledge (Jñānarūpa, ज्ञानरूप). Katha Upaniṣad reiterates the same fact -

तमेव भान्तं अनुभाति सर्वं तस्य भासा सर्वमिदं विभाति ।

*Tameva bhāntaṁ anubhāti sarvaṁ*

*Tasya bhāsā sarvamidaṁ vibhāti // (5-15)*

- The self-luminous light of Ātman i.e. Pure Knowledge, is the main reason why every knowable entity is known by the knower.

All objects shine (are known) only in the light of Pure Consciousness (Ātman). Ātman (Puruṣa, पुरुष) is the illuminor (Prakāśaka, प्रकाशक) while everything else is illumined (Prakāśya, प्रकाश्य).

The treatise of Dṛk-Dṛśya Viveka clearly states -

कामः संकल्पसंदेहौ श्रद्धाऽश्रद्धे धृतीतरे ।

ह्रीर्धीर्भीरित्येवमादीन् भासयत्येकधा चितिः ॥ ४ ॥

*Kāmaḥ saṅkalpa sandehou śraddhā'śraddhe dhṛtītare /*

*Hrīrdhīrbhīrityevamādin bhāsayatyekadhā citiḥ // 4 //*

- (Traits of the mind such as) Desires, resolves, doubts, faith, skepticism, grit, modesty, understanding, fear are illumined by only one Pure Consciousness (Ātman).

The illuminor cannot be the same as the illumined. So, it is not possible for Ātman (I) to be the same as the body.

St. Tukārāma says that once the body is refuted in deep meditation, one can realize Ātman as his real Self.

## Body and Jīva are separate as per Karmakanda

प्रोक्तोऽपि कर्मकाण्डेन ह्यात्मा देहाद्विलक्षणः ।
नित्यश्च तत्फलं भुङ्क्ते देहपातादनन्तरम् ॥ ३८ ॥

*Prokto'pi Karmakāṇḍena hyātmā dehādvilakṣāṇaḥ /*
*Nityaśca tatphalaṁ bhuṅkte dehapātādanataram // 38 //*

**Meaning:** Also, in the Karmakāṇḍa (कर्मकाण्ड) chapter of the Vedas, it is mentioned that Ātman is separate from the body. It bears the results of actions (done in this birth) even after death of the body. So how can Ātman be the same as the body?

The word Karmakāṇḍa stands for the section in Vedas that discuss the theory of executing actions in the best possible manner to be able to go to the heaven after death.

Vedas consist of two sections:

- **PurvaMīmāṅsa** (पूर्वमीमांसा) - Karmakāṇḍa (the section of actions) was elaborated by Jaimini in PurvaMīmāṅsa. When Jīva performs actions like yajñā, donations etc. as prescribed in Vedas, he goes to heaven (Swarga) and enjoys plush luxuries. This is the highest goal of PurvaMīmāṅsa**.** Going to heaven is just like Mokṣa for them. Entire theory of Karmakāṇḍa is based on this aim.
- **UttaraMīmāṅsa** (उत्तरमीमांसा) - Sage Śri Vyāsa wrote Brahmasūtra or UttaraMīmāṅsa, which refuted all other schools of thoughts and various theories including

PurvaMīmāṅsa. When Jīva performs actions in a selfless manner, his mind is purified, and he becomes eligible for acquiring the ultimate Knowledge of Ātman mentioned in Upaniṣads about attaining Mokṣa (liberation).

Thus, Jīva goes to Swarga and comes back from it as per one theory or, Jīva gets liberated from the body as per the other theory. Either way, it is clearly separate from the body. Vedānta uses the term Jivātmā in the context of bondage or liberation, however, once liberated it is known as Ātman or Kuṭastha-Caitanya (कूटस्थ चैतन्य). Thus, the fact that Ātman is separate from the body is known and accepted everywhere (in all systems).

## Subtle body is not Ātman as well

**लिङ्गं चानेकसंयुक्तं चलं दृश्यं विकारि च ।**

**अव्यापकमसद्रूपं तत्कथं स्यात्पुमानयम् ॥ ३९ ॥**

*Liṅgam cānekasaṁyuktam calaṁ dṛsyaṁ vikāri ca /*

*Avyāpakamasadrūpaṁ tatkathaṁ syātpumānayam //39 //*

**Meaning:** The subtle body consists of many elements. It is changeable, unstable and known by Jīva. How can the subtle body, bounded and limited, be the same as Ātman?

Subtle body is made up of 24 different elements -

- 5 Great elements (Pañca-Mahābhūta, पंचमहाभूते)
    - Earth (Pṛthvī, पृथ्वी)
    - Water (Āpa, आप)
    - Fire (Teja, तेज)

    - Wind (Vāyū, वायू)
    - Sky (Ākāśa, आकाश)
- 5 Sense organs (Pañca-Jñanendriya, पंचज्ञानेंद्रिये)
    - Nose (Ghrāṇa, घ्राण)
    - Tongue (Jihvā, जिह्वा)
    - Eyes (Chakṣu, चक्षु)
    - Skin (Tvak, त्वक्)
    - Ear (Śrotra, श्रोत्र)
- 5 Action organs (Pañca-Karmendriya, पंचकर्मेंद्रिये)
    - Rectum (Pāyū, पायू)
    - Genitals (Upastha, उपस्थ)
    - Feet (Pāda, पाद)
    - Hands (Pāṇi, पाणि)
    - Mouth (Vāk, वाक्)
- 5 Life forces (Pañca-Prāṇa, पंचप्राण)
    - Prāṇa (प्राण)
    - Apāna (अपान)
    - Udāna (उदान)
    - Samāna (समान)
    - Vyāna (व्यान)
- Antaḥkaraṇa (अंतःकरण)
    - Ego (Ahaṅkāra, अहंकार)
    - Memory (Citta, चित्त)
    - Intellect (Buddhi, बुद्धि)
    - Mind (Manas, मन)

Ātman is formless as well as organless. It has no break, division or separation of any kind; so obviously Ātman cannot be the same as the subtle body. All elements of the subtle body are unstable, impermanent. Jīva acquires knowledge of those elements. Ātman is neither the knower nor the knowable. All elements of the subtle body are limited to a body-mind system, so how can they be the same as Ātman?

## Conclusion

**एवं देहद्वयादन्य आत्मा पुरुष ईश्वरः ।**

**सर्वात्मा सर्वरूपश्च सर्वातीतोऽहमव्ययः ॥ ४० ॥**

*Evaṁ dehadvayādanya Ātmā Puruṣa Īśvaraḥ /*

*Sarvātmā sarvarūpaśca sarvātīto'hamavyayaḥ // 40 //*

**Meaning:** Thus, Ātman is separate from the gross body and subtle body. It is all-pervasive yet detached from everything. It is present in every form, and it is Īśvara (the Self of all). It is changeless and the substratum of I (ego).

Ātman pervades the gross body made of flesh and bones. It also pervades the subtle body that consists of mind, intellect, memory etc. Yet, Ātman transcends both the gross body and the subtle body. It is the Supreme principle, which exists inside every being in the form of 'I'. It appears to be manifested in the form of all visible objects, yet it remains detached from them. It is changeless and immutable. In 'Soham' meditation:

| **Word** (Pada, पद) | **Explicit meaning** (Vacyartha, वाच्यार्थ) | **Implicit meaning** (Lakṣyartha, लक्ष्यार्थ) |
|---|---|---|
| **Saha** (सः) | Īśvara (ईश्वर) | Brahman (ब्रह्म) |

| **Aham** (अहं) | Jīva (जीव) | Ātman (Kutastha Caitanya, कूटस्थ चैतन्य) |
|---|---|---|

In the process of meditation, the seeker realizes that Jīva is One with Brahman.

Ātman is the 'I'ness of 'I'. It is also called as Puruṣa, since it stays in body, which is a town (Pura) with nine gates. One Ātman (Brahman) pervades completely in millions of species. The bodies may change, but Ātman remains the same without change or mutation of any kind.

## One Explanation

**इत्यात्मदेहभानेन प्रपञ्चस्यैव सत्यता ।**
**यथोक्ता तर्कशास्त्रेण ततः किं पुरुषार्थता ॥ ४१ ॥**
*Ityātmadehabhānena prapañcasyaiva satyatā /*
*Yathoktā tarkaśāstreṇa tataḥ kiṁ puruṣārthatā // 41 //*
**इत्यात्मदेहभेदेन देहात्मत्वं निवारितम् ।**
**इदानीं देहभेदस्य ह्यसत्त्वं स्फुटमुच्यते ॥ ४२॥**
*Ityātmadehabhedena dehātmatvaṁ nivāritam /*
*Idānīṁ dehabhedasya hyasatvaṁ sphuṭamucyate // 42 //*

**Meaning:** So far, by stating the difference between the body and Ātman, only the reality of the worldly life is explained. The theory based on logic (*Tarkaśāstra*, तर्कशास्त्र) discusses the same difference as well. So, is there anything new to learn (in this treatise)? The answer to this question is - by stating the difference between body and Ātman, we have only refuted the opponents, who hold the theory that 'body is Ātman'. Now we will prove that the body, which was stated to be different from Ātman, has no seperate existence in reality.

Using the theory of 'false attribution' (Adhyāropa), it was assumed in the beginning that the body has real existence. By assuming its existence, the body was shown to be different from Ātman in many ways [Verse 17-21 and 31-37]. The existence of the body is generally assumed to be real by most people. This assumption was kept intact in the beginning and Ātman was separated from the body. Now, we will prove that 'the body itself is not real' i.e. the body does not have an autonomous existence. The distinction of the theory of Kevala Advaita lies precisely in this point from other schools such as Dualism or Nyāyaśāstra etc. This realization that 'the body is not real' is the highest achievement (*Puruṣartha*, पुरुषार्थ) of human life.

## Body has no separate, autonomous existence

**चैतन्यस्यैकरूपत्वाद्भेदो युक्तो न कर्हिचित् ।**
**जीवत्वं च मृषा ज्ञेयं रज्ज्वां सर्पग्रहो यथा ॥ ४३ ॥**

*Caitanyasyaikarūpatvadbhedo yukto na karhicit |*
*Jīvatvaṁ ca mṛshā jñeyaṁ rajjvāṁ sarpagraho yathā || 43 ||*

**Meaning:** Pure Consciousness is always the only One principle, which has no division of any kind. Thus, it is unwise and delusional to assume the separate existence of Jīva, just as it is wrong to perceive the separate existence of a snake on a rope.

Upaniṣads firmly propound that Brahman is One, monolithic, indivisible and formless.

रसो वै सः ।

Raso vai saḥ / *(Tai. Up. 2.7)*

- Brahman is the essence of the entire creation. It is Bliss itself.

एकधातुर्द्रष्टव्यं ।

*Ekadhāturdraṣṭavyam / (Chān. Up. 6.2.1)*

- Brahman has no differences, distinctions (Bheda, भेद) of any of the three kinds [See verse 35].

All saints propound the same fact through their texts. St. Jñāneśwara says –

भरला घनदाट हरी दिसे ।

*Bharala ghanadāṭa Hari dise /*

- I see the God permeating everything around me.

This fact can be understood well with the help of utmomst faith in Vedāntic scriptures, Sadguru, and logical analysis. Ātman is Pure Consciousness (Caitanya), which is only One. So, dividing it into various sections such as JīvaCaitanya (individual consciousness), ĪśvaraCaitanya (universal consciousness), or JadaCaitanya (consiousness in insentient objects) does not conform to logic.

Katha Upaniṣad says -

नेह नानास्ति किञ्चन ।

*Neha nānāsti kiñcana / (Bru. Up.)*

- There are no parts or divisions in Brahman. Other than Brahman, nothing else exists.

This is the official scriptural analysis of Brahman. However, the world is full of many Jīvas, divisions and differences. These differences are addressed systematically in Vedānta in two ways -

- The theory of 'false attribution' (Adhyāropa, अध्यारोप) - This states that the world is a 'false superimposition' (Adhyāsta) on the substratum of (Adhiṣṭhāna) Brahman.
- The concept of limiting adjunct (Upādhi, उपाधी) - This states that the visible world is a limiting adjunct of Brahman. The world is full of many sentient and insentient entities. However, Brahman is verily the only One. It permeates the world and beyond yet remains detached from everything.

There are many theories in Vedānta that explain the relation between Brahman and the world -

- Nisargavāda (निसर्गवाद) - The world exists and functions automatically. There is no other regulator or substratum of the world other than the nature itself.
- Īśvarakāraṇavāda (ईश्वरकारणवाद) - God is the creator of the world. He regulates it, maintains it and destroys it as well.
- Māyāvāda (मायावाद) - Māyā is an imaginary power. Brahman + Māyā = Īśvara. Īśvara regulates the world with the help of Māyā.
- Jalataraṅgavāda (जलतरंगवाद) - The world appears in Brahman just like ripples, waves appear in the ocean.
- Sarvabrahmavāda (सर्वब्रह्मवाद) - Everything in this world is verily Brahman, nothing else.

- Ajātavāda (अजातवाद) - The world is never born. It has no existence in past, present, future. Only Brahman is real.
- Vastūprabhāvāda (वस्तूप्रभावाद) - The world is the shining glory or resplendence of Brahman.

One of the classic examples in Vedānta says that a snake is delusively perceived on a rope when seen in partial darkness. There are three ways in which this illusive appearance can be explained -

- A snake is seen instead of a rope
- A snake is seen on a rope
- A snake is seen in the place of a rope

However, in darkness, one only sees the snake and no rope. Only when a light is thrown on the rope, the observer understands that the snake was seen on (in the place of / instead of) the rope. Until one knows the rope, he falsely perceives the snake as real and feels scared. The perceived snake is always the rope and nothing else. The snake has no autonomous existence.

Similarly, the visible world and all entities are always Brahman and nothing else. However, until one gains Pure Knowledge of Brahman, he delusively thinks that the world is real just the way it seems. There are other examples in Vedānta similar to the snake and rope -

- **Seashell-Silver** (Śukti-Rajat, शुक्ति-रजत) - A seashell in a beach starts glittering in bright sunlight, and there is an illusion of silver lying in the sand instead of the seashell.

- **Bare tree trunk-Person** (Sthāṇu-Puruṣa, स्थाणू-पुरूष) - At dusk-time, a bare-tree trunk looks like a person due to partial darkness.

Just like all these examples, the world is delusively seen instead of Brahman in the darkness of ignorance.

Vedānta also explains this concept using the state of dream. While dreaming, a person feels that everything in a dream is very real. He may feel very happy, sad, hungry, thirsty or scared in the dream. However, all objects and experiences in dream become moot when one gets up from sleep. Similarly, the diversified world in our present experience is a result of being asleep in ignorance (Ajñāna). When a seeker awakens to the Pure, Absolute Knowledge of Brahman, all variations and differences in the world disappear in Brahman (become inconsequential).

A rope and a snake both cannot be seen at the same time in the same place on the substratum of each other. A snake is seen with a specific color, size or movements in ignorance. But these attributes do not apply to a rope after one gains the knowledge of the rope.

In the beginning, one gains only the general knowledge of the base object (rope) - 'it (something) is there'. This is termed as Idanta (इदंता). Later, there is specific knowledge of the illusive snake - 'it is a snake'. Due to the specific knowledge of the snake, the initial general knowledge of the rope is eradicated. A person gets deluded due to the combination of convoluted shape, length, width, partial darkness, and fear. Ignorance of a real object (rope) is the main reason for seeing false appearance of the snake. When the rope is seen as real in the light, it is the Truth (Satya). This is known as Sākṣātkāra (साक्षात्कार) i.e. seeing something openly for real. With this knowledge of the rope, illusion of the snake is eradicated. Sākṣātkāra (seeing for real) is the characteristic property of knowledge. Because of this property, ignorance, which is the very obstacle in the path of knowledge, is wiped out.

Seeing the rope as a snake and seeing Ātman as a body are both examples of ignorance. Seeing Pure Consciousness as insentience is the height of ignorance. Ignorance is eradicated only with the knowledge.

## Appearance of multiplicity is due to ignorance

रज्ज्वज्ञानात्क्षणेनैव यद्वद्रज्जुर्हि सर्पिणी ।
भाति तद्वच्चितिः साक्षाद्विश्वाकारेण केवला ॥ ४४ ॥

*Rajjvajñānātkṣāṇenaiva yadvadrajjurhi sarpiṇi /*
*Bhāti tadvaccitiḥ sakṣādviśvākāreṇa kevala // 44 //*

**Meaning:** The illusive appearance of a snake is possible only when there is ignorance of the rope. Similarly, the illusion of multiple forms is possible only when there is ignorance of Pure Consciousness.

The only way to realize the ultimate Truth (Satya, सत्य) is AparokṣaJñāna (direct cognition) of the Truth. One wrongly imagines the appearance of many names and forms instead of the One Truth. For e.g. when a rope lies in darkness, one may see a snake or a garland or a crack in the floor or streamlet lying in the same place. The very nature of the mind is to imagine; hence, mind cannot be a tool for realizing the ultimate Truth (Satya). Intellect is expert at logical analysis, however it is tainted with many memories and subtle imprints. So, even intellect cannot research the ultimate Truth. Instead, it imagines the presence of enormous names and forms in One Ātman. Yogavasiṣṭha (योगवासिष्ठ) says -

**पंचभूतात्मकम् विश्वं मरीचिजलसन्निभम् ।**

*Pañcabhūtātmakam Viśvam marīcijalasannibham /*

- The world which is made up of the five great elements is as imaginary as a mirage in a desert.

Ādi Śaṅkarācārya, in his commentary, says -

**अध्यारोपितनामरूपकर्मद्वारेण ब्रह्म निर्दिश्यते ।** *(Bri. Up. 2.3.6)*

*Adhyāropita nāma rūpa karmadwāreṇa Brahma nirdiśyate /*

- We can infer the presence of Brahman whenever a name or a form or an activity is seen.

One can fully assimilate these teachings with the help of the study of Upaniṣads.

## Brahman is the 'material cause' of the universe

**उपादानं प्रपञ्चस्य ब्रह्मणोऽन्यन्न विद्यते ।**
**तस्मात्सर्वप्रपञ्चोऽयं ब्रह्मैवास्ति न चेतरत् ॥ ४५ ॥**

*Upādānaṁ prapañcasya Brahmano'anynna vidyate /*
*Tasmātsarvaprapañco'yaṁ Brahmaivāsti na cetarat // 45 //*

**Meaning:** Brahman is the only 'material cause' (Upādāna Karaṇa) of the universe. Hence, everything in this universe is Brahman and nothing else.

This is the pinnacle of Indian doctrine and philosophy. This is precisely the teaching of Kevala Advaita school of Vedānta. There may be many schools of thought in Indian philosophy, however, Kevala Advaita is generally accepted by majority of the people. Most enlightened saints have embraced it with absolute certainty. The doctrine of Kevala Advaita is based on Ādi Śaṅkarācārya's commentary on Upaniṣads, Brahmasūtras, and Bhagvad-Gītā.

The clay is the 'material cause' of all (earthern) pots. It means that the clay (cause) exists in all pots (effect). Similarly, Brahman (cause) exists in all elements of the universe (effect). Brahman and the universe are One. So, the cause-effect relationship between them is imaginary in nature.

There is a verse in Chāndogya Upaniṣad -

एकोऽहम् बहुस्याम् ।

*Eko'ham bahusyām / (6.2.3)*

- (Brahman thinks) I am one and I shall manifest in many forms.

Vedānta states that the universe is created from this instinctive thought of Brahman. According to Vedānta, this instinct is imaginary so the universe (created out of the instinct) is imaginary as well.

Brahman is also the 'instrumental cause' (Nimitta Kāraṇa, निमित्त कारण) of the universe. Brahman is one, so it cannot possibly be different as a 'material cause' and an 'instrumental cause'. This is the reason why it is known as AbhinnaNimittaUpādānaKāraṇa (अभिन्ननिमित्तउपादानकारण, single undivided 'material cause' and 'instrumental cause') of the universe.

Upaniṣad says -

सत एव सौम्य इदमग्र आसीत ।

*Sat eva somya idamagra āsit / (Chan. Up. 6.2.1)*

- Only Sat (Brahman) existed before the beginning of this universe.

एकमेवाद्वितीयम् ।

*Ekamevādvitiyam / (Chan. Up. 6.2.1)*

- Only One and free from duality.

According to these verses, Sat-Cit-Ānanda Brahman appears as if it is manifested in the form of the universe. In other words, it does not have a real existence. Hence, sentient and insentient entities do not have an independent existence. The unreal world appears to be real only due to ignorance. One cannot know or learn Sat so long as he thinks that the world is real. With deep studies of scriptures, one gains the Pure Knowledge of Brahman. As a result, ignorance is eradicated, and the seeker says instinctively -

अहं ब्रह्मास्मि ।

*Aham Brahmāsmi / (Bru. Up. 1.14.10)*

- I am Brahman

सर्वं खल्विदं ब्रह्म ।

*Sarvaṁ khalvidaṁ Brahman / (Chan. Up. 3.14.1)*

- All objects indicated by I / mine, and this / that are Brahman in essence.

## Pervaded and pervader analysis -

व्याप्यव्यापकता मिथ्या सर्वमात्मेति शासनात् ।
इति ज्ञाते परे तत्त्वे भेदस्यावसरः कुतः ॥ ४६ ॥

*Vyāpyavyāpakatā Mithyā sarvamātmeti śāsanāt /*
*Iti jñāte pare tatve bhedasyāvasaraḥ kutaḥ // 46 //*

**Meaning:** Everything is Brahman and Brahman is all-pervading. Hence, the idea of pervaded and pervader is illusory (Mithyā). When the subtle principle (Brahman) is realized, where is the room for distinction or division of any kind?

The word Sarvavyāpi (सर्वव्यापी) denotes that Brahman pervades everything. It also leads to erroneous thinking that the world gets pervaded (Vyāpya, व्याप्य), while one that pervades (Vyāpaka, व्यापक) is Brahman, so dualism is real. To address this issue, another Śruti describes Brahman as -

ओतश्च प्रोतश्च ।

*Otaśca protaśca / (Nru. Tap. Vol. 8)*

- (One which is) filled completely inside and outside, without any space in between (is Brahman).

This again leads to incorrect thinking that there is a division of inside and outside (w.r.t. Brahman). It results in the delusion that one that pervades (Brahman) has a separate, autonomous existence. Munḍaka Upaniṣad has a similar Śruti in this regard -

सबाह्याभ्यन्तरोह्यजः ।

*Sabhyābhyāntarohyajaḥ / (2.1.2)*

- This birthless God pervades us inside out.

All differences (in the world) are seen as real due to ignorance. Vedānta uses the theory of 'false attribution' (Adhyāropa), to temporarily explain the difference between in and out, pervaded and pervading. That the diversified appearance of the world is real is called as Adhyāropa. However, it is only for preliminary understanding of the seeker. This understanding is subsequently refuted (Apavāda), and it is proved that Brahman alone is real.

Katha Upaniṣad has a Mantra that explains Brahman in this verse -

तमेव भान्तं अनुभाति सर्वं तस्य भासा सर्वमिदं विभाति ।

*Tameva bhāntaṁ anubhāti sarvaṁ tasya bhāsā sarvamidaṁ vibhāti / (5.15)*

- The self-luminous light of Ātman i.e. Pure Knowledge, is the one that illumines everything else in the world (It is the light due to which every knowable entity is known by the knower.)

Here again, Upaniṣad temporarily accepts the difference of illuminor (Brahman) and illumined (world).

The imprints (Saṅskāra, संस्कार) of difference or division are so deeply rooted in human psyche, that duality must be accepted as real in the beginning only to refute it later.

Kena Upaniṣad describes Brahman as -

यन्मनसा न मनुते येनाहुर्मनो मतम् ।

तदेव ब्रह्म त्वं विद्धि नेदं यदिदमुपासते ॥

*Yanmanasā na manute yenāhurmanomatam /*

*Tadeva Brahma tvaṁ viddhi nedaṁ yadidamupāsate // (1.1.5)*

- Brahman cannot be comprehended by the mind, but it is Brahman that gives the mind its thinking capability.

Sadguru does not know how to explain Brahman to disciples, since without accepting diversified appearance of the world (Adhyāropa), it is impossible to discuss anything.

Now we can discuss the concepts of inside and outside, objects denoted by this and that, pervader and pervaded etc. In this same verse, Ācārya uses the word **Mithyā** (मिथ्या) to explain imaginary differences seen in the world. Vedānta uses the term **Sat-Asat Vilakṣāna Anirvachaniya** (सत् असत् विलक्षण अनिर्वचनीय), which means (variegated appearance of) the world is neither 'real' nor 'unreal', hence 'indescribable'.

The word **Sat** or Satya means Pure Existence irrespective of the past, present or future. Sat is the one that stays unaltered in all three times. But, the world changes with time. It did not exist many million years ago in the past, it exists now, and it will cease to exist sometime in future. Existence of the world is pertinent to the time. Hence it is not Sat i.e. it is **Sat-contradictory** (Sat-Vilakṣāṇa, सत् विलक्षण).

- The word **Asat** means absolute or Pure Non-existence. Asat or Asatya means that, which has no existence at any given time. Asat can never be seen or perceived by anyone. Vedānta puts forth the three famous examples of Asat: the sky flower (khapushpa, खपुष्प), horns of a hare (śaśaśṛṅga, शशश्रुंग) and son of a sterile woman (vandhyā-putra, वंध्यापुत्र). The world cannot be called as Asat, since it can be perceived at present. It does not match the definition of Asat i.e. it is **Asat-contradictory** (Asat-Vilakṣāṇa, असत् विलक्षण).
- The world is neither Sat nor Asat i.e. Sat-Asat-Contradictory, and hence indescribable (Anirvachaniya, अनिर्वचनीय) and illusive (Mithyā, मिथ्या).

The world is perceived as real due to ignorance. However, with knowledge that 'everything is Brahman', the sense of reality is eradicated from the mind. Thus, the world has but an illusive appearance (Mithyā, मिथ्या). All enlightened saints, sages and seers promote the same fact. After Self-realization, when one learns that the world is illusive, its external appearance and all differences (in, out, this, that etc.) continue to exist for all practical purposes. Even enlightened people lead their day-to-day life as per their destiny (Prārabdha, प्रारब्ध). However, the worldly events, miseries, griefs, conflicts stop being troublesome since the sense of reality in the world is eradicated for them.

## Upaniṣad Eradicates all differences -

श्रुत्या निवारितं नूनं नानात्वं स्वमुखेन हि ।

कथं भासो भवेदन्यः स्थिते चाद्वयकारणे ॥ ४७ ॥

*Śrutyā nivāritaṁ nūnaṁ nānātvaṁ swamukhena hi /*

*Kathaṁ bhāso bhāvedanyaḥ sthite cādvaya kāraṇe // 47 //*

**Meaning:** Upaniṣads themselves eradicate the manifoldness of the world with their verses. Brahman is non-dual and the only One (that is real), so how could the phenomenal world be different form it.

There are many verses in Upaniṣads that refute the false appearance of diversity in the world. For example:

नेह नानास्ति किञ्चन ।

*Neha nānāsti kiñcan / (Katha Up. 2.1.11)*

- There are no parts or divisions in Brahman. Other than Brahman, nothing else exists.

The verses of Śruti should be accepted as final and authoritative in the matter of knowledge. The theory of Upaniṣads has been irrefuted so far. Saint poet Laxmidhara calls the Śruti verses as Katakṣā (कटाक्ष) in his text Advita Makaranda. Śraddha (श्रद्धा, spiritual faith) involves utmost, unwavering faith in the verses of Upaniṣads. Even the composition of Bhagvad-Gītā is based in Upaniṣads. All saints and enlightened seers accept Śruti as the final authoritative scriptures, and their compositions reflect the teachings of Upaniṣads.

## The result of seeing differences

दोषोऽपि विहितः श्रुत्या मृत्योर्मृत्युं स गच्छति ।

इह पश्यति नानात्वं मायया वञ्चितो नरः ॥ ४८ ॥

*Dosho'pi vihitaḥ śrutyā mṛtyormṛtyum sa gaccati |*
*Iha paśyati nanātvam Māyaya vañcito naraḥ || 48 ||*

**Meaning:** One who is deluded by Māyā sees manifoldness in the world. As a result of this delusion, he (continuously) goes from one death to the other.

Katha Upaniṣad mentions this verse –

मृत्योः स मृत्युं गच्छति य इह नानेव पश्यति ।

*Mṛtyoḥ sa mṛtyūmgacchati ya iha nāneva paśyati | (2.1.11)*

- One who sees differences in this world, leads himself from one death to another (he goes through continuous life-death cycle).

To go from one death to the other, one obviously needs to first go from one birth to the other. The reason for seeing manifoldness is the ignorance that 'body is the real self i.e. I (Ātman)'. There is no bigger ignorance than thinking that there are as many Ātmans as there are bodies. The ignorance that 'I am the body' also leads to the thinking that 'he is a body'. Manifoldness becomes unbounded with this thinking. There are many bodies in many different species (humans, birds, animals etc.) and diversity pervades everywhere. As a result of diversity, 'me and mine', 'you and yours' thinking evolves. It further leads to jealousy, competition, enmity, love, attachment, repentence, worry and mineness. Māyā proliferates everywhere in this manner. Revenge, violence and treachery are the highest manifestations of Māyā, which leave no scope for spiritual thoughts about liberation (Mokṣa). Insentient, visible, perishable and illuminable world is incorrectly perceived as real, and one develops attachment towards it. Jīva gets involved in the worldly activities and gets caught in the web of continuous life-death.

Praśnopaniṣad says that by seeing only One Brahman everywhere, one doesn't feel scared of the death.

अरा इव रथनाभौ कला यस्मिन् प्रतिष्ठिताः ।
तं वेद्यं पुरुषं वेद यथा मा वो मृत्युः परीव्यथा इति ॥ *(6.6)*

*Arā iva rathanābhau kalā yasmin pratiṣṭhitāḥ /*
*Taṁ vedyaṁ Puruṣaṁ veda yathā mā vo mṛtyuh parivyathā iti //*

- Like the spokes of the wheel, which meet at one center, all differences (variations) meet in One Puruṣa (Ātman). Know that Ātman and consequently, you will not be troubled by death. Enormous manifoldness meets in one place. Know that One place of unity.

## The world is created from Brahman

ब्रह्मणः सर्वभूतानि जायन्ते परमात्मनः ।
तस्मादेतानि ब्रह्मैव भवन्तीत्यवधारयेत् ॥ ४९ ॥

*Brahmaṇaḥ sarvabhūtāni jāyante paramātmanaḥ /*
*Tasmādetāni Brahmaiva bhāvantītyavadhārayet // 49 //*

**Meaning:** All living beings come into existence from Brahman. Hence, one should deterministically know that everyone is verily Brahman.

Taittirīya Upaniṣad proclaims that -

यतो व इमानि भूतानि जायन्ते ।

*Yato va imāni bhūtāni jāyante / (3.1.1)*

- That from which these beings are born (is Brahman).

Bhagvad-Gītā says that -

मत्तः परतरं नान्यत् किञ्चिदस्ति ।

*Mattaḥ parataraṁ nānyat kiñcidasti* | *(7.7)*

- There is nothing, not even slightest (entity) that is different from Me (Brahman)

Chāndogya Upaniṣad says that -

सत् एव सोम्य इदमग्र आसीत् ।

*Sat eva somya idamagra āsit* | *(6.2.1)*

- Only Sat (Brahman) existed before the beginning of this universe.

- All entities in the universe are created from Sat (Brahman), hence they are all Sat. Brahman does not turn into the worldly objects like metal is turned into coins in a mint. Coins are created methodically in a mint by a separate creator. However, Brahman itself manifests (Vivarta, विवर्त) in the form of all sentient and insentient entities. Seeing the continuous presence of Brahman everywhere is called as Anvaya (अन्वय).
- Another verse in Vedānta says that, the world is created instantly in one flash (Yugapat, युगपत्).
- The theory of Pariṇamavāda (परिणामवाद) states that, the world is a changed version of Brahman the way milk changes into curd.
- Jalataraṅgavāda (जलतरंगवाद) states that, all entities that appear in Brahman are like ripples that appear in water.

It is right to accept the theory of Vivartavāda (विवर्तवाद), Māyāvāda (मायावाद) or Vastūprabhāvāda (वस्तूप्रभावाद).

Sentient beings have a mind with Cidābhāsa (Reflected Consciousness), while insentient objects do not have the mind (Antaḥkaraṇa). Sentient beings have a physical and subtle body, while insentient entities only have a physical form. While drawing a picture on paper, one may draw insentient objects like stones, water, mountains as well as sentient beings like birds, anials, trees etc. However, all of them are nothing but paper and color. Similarly, all sentient and insentient entities are nothing but Māyā as stated in Pañcadashi (6.2). In Jalataraṅgavāda, ripples are made up of water, so it is not possible to differentiate between sentient and insentient entities in it. However, that distinction is seen clearly in the example of colored picture on paper.

## All-pervasive Brahman

**ब्रह्मैव सर्वनामानि रूपाणि विविधानि च ।**

**कर्माण्यपि समग्राणि बिभर्तीति श्रुतिर्जगौ ॥ ५० ॥**

*Brahmaiva sarva nāmāni rūpāṇi vividhāni ca /*

*Karmāṇyapi samagrāṇi bibhartīti śrutirjagou // 50 //*

**Meaning**: Śruti has clearly declared that Brahman has as if manifested through all names and forms. All kinds of actions are Brahman as well.

Ādi Śaṅkarācārya says -

**अध्यारोपितनामरूपकर्मद्वारेण ब्रह्म निर्दिश्यते ।**

*Adhyāropita nāma rūpa karmadwāreṇa Brahma nirdiśyate / (Bri. Up. Commentary 2.3.6)*

- We can infer the presence of Brahman whenever a name or a form or an activity is seen.

Praśna Upaniṣad says -

**स प्राणमसृजत । प्राणाच्छ्रद्धां खं वायुर्ज्योतिरापः पृथिवीन्द्रियं मनोऽन्नमन्नाद्वीर्यं तपो मन्त्राः कर्मलोका लोकेषु च नाम च ॥**

*Sa Prāṇamasrujata / Prāṇacchraddham kham vayurjyotirapah prithivindriyam mano'nnamannaviryam tapo mantrah karma loka lokeshu ca nama ca // (6.4)*

- Īśvara first created Prāṇa. From Prāṇa faith (Śraddha, श्रद्धा), then sky, wind, fire, water, clay, organs, mind and food (were created). From food, power (of progenity), austere practices (Tapas, तप), Mantra, actions and various plains (Loka, लोक) were created. Many names were created in these plains. Names, forms and actions are all parts of this Puruṣa, who is made up of sixteen sections (kalā, कला). The Puruṣa was created from but one thought (Saṅkalpa, संकल्प) of Brahman.

This theory of creation of the universe from Brahman is 'false attribution' (Adhyāropa). One should learn and remember this sequence Prāṇa → Food → Actions → Plains → Names. Note that the process of creation of universe may be different in another system. These various theories are created so that a seeker can meditate in reverse order and unite with The Creator.

Ādi Śaṅkarācārya has explained this in detail in his commentary on the Brahmasūtra –

**जन्माद्यस्य यतः ।**

*Janmādyasya yataḥ / (1.1.2)*

- (Ātman is that) from which the origin, sustenance and dissolution of this (world derive).

## The unity between the world and Brahman

सुवर्णाज्जायमानस्य सुवर्णत्वञ्च शाश्वतम् ।

ब्रह्मणो जायमानस्य ब्रह्मत्वं च तथा भवेत् ॥ ५१ ॥

*Suvarṇājjāyamānasya suvarṇatvañca śāśvatam /*

*Brahmano jāyamānasya Brahmatvam ca tathā bhāvet // 51 //*

**Meaning:** Gold exists perpetually in all ornaments made up of gold. Similarly, Brahman exists perpetually in all entities in this world that itself is created from Brahman.

If ornaments are created from gold and melted again, then they lose their specific form and name. However, the gold remains as is. Similarly, irrespective of how many entities are created and destroyed in the world, Brahman remains as is. St. Jñāneśwara says -

सुवर्णाचे मणी केले । ते सोनियाचे सुतीं वोविले ।

*Suvarṇache mani kele / Te Soniyache suti vovile / (7.32)*

- Golden beads are woven in the golden thread.

This means that all worldly entities made from Brahman are connected by Brahman itself. A blind person must follow the directions given by a person with eyes and tread on the same path. Similarly, people who are (spiritually) ignorant must follow the verses in Upaniṣads and think accordingly. Ice is made up of nothing else but water. Pots of all sizes, shapes and colors are made up of only clay. Similarly, the world consists of only Pure Existence-Consciousness-Bliss (Brahman) and nothing else. Munḍaka Upaniṣad (1.1.3) states that when one knows iron, it is as if one understands all objects made of iron.

## Fear due to duality

स्वल्पमप्यन्तरं कृत्वा जीवात्मपरमात्मनोः ।
योऽवतिष्ठति मूढात्मा भयं तस्याभिभाषितम् ॥ ५२ ॥

*Swalpamapyantaraṁ kṛtvā Jivātmaparamātmanoḥ /*
*Yo'vatiṣṭhati mūḍhātmā bhayam tasyābhibhāṣitam // 52 //*

**Meaning:** Even if a trace of separation is left between Jivātmā and Paramātmā, the ignorant person (who makes such distinction) gets defeated by fear.

This verse is based on Bṛhadāraṇyaka Upaniṣad -

द्वितीयाद्वै भयं भवति ।

*Dvitīyādvai bhayaṁ bhāvati / (1.4.2)*

- Where there is a second, there is fear.

The word 'fear' is always in the context of some other person, object, event or circumstance. People, objects, events are inherently separate or distinct from each other. Sometimes a person feels scared of himself. E.g. one may feel scared that I might hurt someone, or I might ruin something, or there might be an event that will invite a series of troubles in life. If a person is inflicted with cancer, he feels scared of cancer (which is technically separate from himself). Because of cancer, I will die, and I will have to leave my body and all my belongings in the world - this is the real fear that lies underneath the fear of cancer. Thus, the ignorance that Ātman (the real Self) is separate from Jīva (the imaginary self) is the foundation of all fears.

Only because one sees duality (differences), enemies and fear are created. Jealousy, hatred, comparison, competition and insecurity are created because one sees manifoldness in the world. These consist of the fear of being unsuccessful, disrespected, sidelined or obsolete w.r.t. others. There is also a fear of the loosing socital status, position and prestige. Everyone is scared of being unhappy, because nobody wants sorrow or misery in life.

All sentient beings have a natural instinct for survival, which leads them to eating food, taking medicines for eradicating diseases, and protecting themselves from heat or cold etc. Even enlightened people perform these activities. However, working for basic survival intuitively vs. fearing the fact that one is unable to do work (due to old age, loneliness, poverty etc.) are two different things. Living life as per natural survival instinct is very different from being scared of death. No enlightened person embraces the death unnecessarily.

## Ignorance is the cause of duality

**यत्राज्ञानाद्भवेद्द्वैतमितरस्तत्र पश्यति ।**
**आत्मत्वेन यदा सर्वं नेतरस्तत्र चाण्वपि ॥ ५३ ॥**

*Yatrājñānadbhaveddvaitamitarastatra paśyati /*
*Ātmatvena yadā sarvaṁ netarastatra cāṇvapi // 53 //*

**Meaning:** Due to the lack of (Pure) Knowledge of Satya (the ultimate Truth), one starts seeing differentiation everywhere. However, when everything is identified with Ātman, one cannot see anything or anyone else at all.

Ātman is the only eternal Truth. One may see enormous differences in people (bodies) and objects. However, all bodies are Upādhi (उपाधी, limiting adjunct) of Brahman, while insentient objects are falsely superimposed (Adhyāsta, अध्यस्त) on Brahman.

Ātman has no Upādhi of any kind, so it is called as Nirūpādhika (निरुपाधिक). All superimposed objects are imagined on the substratum (Adhiṣṭhāna, अधिष्ठान) of Brahman. For the sake of learning and understanding, one may call Pure Consciousness in a body (a single person) as as Ātman and Pure Consciousness pervaded in the world as Brahman. However, body is an object, so it ultimately is a part of all worldly objects. Ātman and Brahman are always One and the same. One sees enormous differentiation in people and objects when one is ignorant about this fact.

Ādi Śaṅkarācārya has started his commentary on Brahmasūtras with this verse -

**युष्मदस्मत्प्रत्ययगोचरयोर्विषयविषयीणोस्तमःप्रकाशवत् विरुद्ध स्वभावयोः ।**

*Yuśmad asmat pratyayagocarayorviśayiṇostamaḥprakāśavat viruddha swabhāvayoḥ* /

- Jīva is completely different from all the objects (that it sees, hears or enjoys) just as light, by nature, is completely different from darkness. Jīva is sentient, while objects are insentient. Sentient is always One, while objects (body, world etc.) are unified in their insentience despite them being different from each other.

St. Jñāneśwara says -

जडाजडीं अंशीं । राहाटे जे सरिसी । ते चेतना गा तुजसी । लटिकें नाहीं ॥

*Jaḍājaḍī anshī / Rāhāṭe je sarisī /*

*Te Cetanā gā tujasī / Laṭike nāhī //* (Jñā.13. 137)

- Brahman equally pervades all sentient and insentient entities in the world.

The universe is divided into sentient and insentient sections for better understanding. However, Pure Consciousness (Brahman) pervades equally in both kinds of entities. The same Pure Consciousness is pervaded in you and me. This is the eternal Truth. Hence, all differentiations or duality that create fear are nothing but imaginary. They are the result of ignorance of the real Self.

## No delusion or grief after Self-realization

यस्मिन्सर्वाणि भूतानि ह्यात्मत्वेन विजानतः ।

न वै तस्य भवेन्मोहो न च शोकोऽद्वितीयतः ॥ ५४ ॥

*Yasminsarvāṇī bhūtāni hyātmatvena vijānataḥ /*

*Na vai tasya bhāvenmoho na ca śoko'dvitīyataḥ // 54 //*

**Meaning:** One who sees Ātman everywhere does not experience any delusion or sorrow because of the absence of duality.

This verse is based on a similar verse in Ishavasya Upaniṣad (7). This and the next verse together indicate the state of an enlightened person, who sees Ātman in everything and everything in Ātman. In this state of non-duality, there is nothing (or none) else that can cause delusion or grief in him. Other similar traits such as affection, hatred, joy, misery etc., are also not felt in the state of non-duality. One can experience (Pure) Bliss that is eternal and independent of anything else. However, only theoretical knowledge of Brahman does not lead to this realization. One needs to strictly evaluate oneself against this criterion.

## Upaniṣad states non-duality

**अयमात्मा हि ब्रह्मैव सर्वात्मकतया स्थितः ।**

**इति निर्धारितं श्रुत्या बृहदारण्यसंस्थया ॥ ५५ ॥**

*Ayamātmā hi Brahmaiva sarvātmakatayā sthitaḥ /*

*Iti nirdhāritaṃ śrutyā Bṛhadāraṇyasaṅsthayā // 55 //*

**Meaning:** Bṛhadāraṇyaka Upaniṣad (and Māṇḍūkya Kārikā) state the fact - Brahman pervades all sentient beings in the form of the Self (Ātman).

The word Sarvātmāka (सर्वात्मक) in this verse has two meanings -

- One who pervades everything
- One who eats everything

The first meaning is more prevalent. Śruti also says that all living and non-living entities disappear in Brahman. In this context, the second meaning is valid as well.

Mahāvākya (महावाक्य) is a sentence that firmly states that Jiva and Brahman are one. This verse mentions one of the four main Mahāvākyas (महावाक्य). There is one Mahāvākya in one Upaniṣad from each of the four Vedas:

| | |
|---|---|
| प्रज्ञानं ब्रह्म ।<br>*Prajñānam Brahma /*<br>*(Rgveda, Aitareya Up.5.3)* | Brahman is the highest and purest form of Knowledge, wisdom and intelligence. |
| अहं ब्रह्मास्मि ।<br>*Aham Brahmāsmi /*<br>*(Yajurveda, Bru. Up. 1.4.10)* | I am Brahman. |
| तत्त्वमसि ।<br>*Tattvamasi /*<br>*(Sāmaveda, Chandogya Up. 6.8.7)* | You are that (Brahman). |
| अयमात्मा ब्रह्म ।<br>*Ayamātmā Brahma /*<br>*(Atharvaveda, Mandukya Up. 2)* | This Ātman is Brahman. |

I am Brahman, this is Brahman, you are Brahman and that is Brahman - in this sequential manner, one can realize all-pervasiveness of Brahman.

## The example of a dream

अनुभूतोऽप्ययं लोको व्यवहारक्षमोऽपि सन् ।
असद्रूपो यथा स्वप्न उत्तरक्षणबाधतः ॥ ५६ ॥
*Anubhūto'pyayaṁ loko vyavahārakṣamo'pi san /*
*Asadṛpo yathā swapna uttarakṣāṇabādhataḥ // 56 //*
स्वप्नो जागरणेऽलीकः स्वप्ने न हि जागरः ।
द्वयमेव लये नास्ति लयोऽपि ह्युभयोर्न च ॥ ५७ ॥
*Swapno jāgaraṇe'likaḥ swapne na hi jagaraḥ /*

*Dvayameva laye nāsti layo'pi hyubhayorna ca || 57 ||*

**Meaning:** Experiences in the waking state are perceived as real in day-to-day life. However, they are as illusive (Mithyā, मिथ्या) as those in the dream world. Experiences in the dream are absent (Vyatireka, व्यतिरेक) in the waking, and experiences in the waking are absent in the dream. Both the states of waking and dream are absent in the deep-sleep, which in-turn is absent in them both.

All experiences in the dream become non-existent in the states of waking and deep-sleep. Hence, it is easy learn that dreams are illusive. Similarly, all experiences in the waking become non-existent in the states of dream and deep-sleep. Still, it is highly difficult to accept the fact that the waking state is as illusive as the dream state. Deep-rooted past Vasanas about the reality of the world are imprinted in the intellect and they do not allow the seeker to be convinced in this way.

Māṇḍūkya Upnishad explains the three states in a beautiful manner. The objects in the waking appear to be continuous and permanent (even when there are intermittent dreams and deep-sleep, where the world and the self cease to exist). This continuity is the main reason why one does not understand the transience or illusiveness of the waking state. However, it is important to learn that all objects, and the person who sees them, are subject to change. The appearance of continuity in the waking is deceiving. Pure Consciousness (Ātman) alone is the eternal Truth. One can notice that the body is ageing fast. But it is not easy to notice that insentient objects are also subject to changes such as rusting, breaking etc. Food items like milk, curd etc. become sour quickly. Platinum is said to have a very long shelf-life; however, it is bound to change or get destroyed after some time. Hence, objects like Platinum should not be considered real (eternal) in nature.

## The three states are illusory

त्रयमेवं भवेन्मिथ्या गुणत्रयविनिर्मितम् ।
अस्य द्रष्टा गुणातीतो नित्यो ह्येकश्चिदात्मकः ॥ ५८ ॥

*Trayamevaṁ bhāvenmithyā guṇatrayavinirmitam /*
*Asya drṣṭā guṇātīto nityo hyekaścidātmākaḥ // 58 //*

**Meaning:** The three states, which are the creation of the three Guṇas, are illusive (Mithyā, मिथ्या), while their Witness Consciousness transcends the three Guṇas. It is eternal (Nitya, नित्य) and the ultimate Truth, since it transcends the past, the present, and the future.

The three states are created from three Guṇas. Guṇas manifest in their own way in the three states.

- Waking - Sattvaguṇa - Clear knowledge (of objects)
- Dream - Rajoguṇa - Random, senseless, flickering, unclear knowledge
- Deep-sleep - Tamoguṇa - No knowledge

The manifestations of each Guṇa change continuously, so it cannot be Ātman (Pure Consciousness). In a long train or flight journey, one may experience the three states interchangeably such as waking, followed by deep-sleep, then a dream followed by waking etc. The order of these three states change as well. Ātman is beyond the three states as mentioned in the Upaniṣad 'Śri Ganapatī Atharvaśīrṣa'. The three Guṇas are created from insentient matter (Prakṛtī, प्रकृती). Hence, Guṇas too, are insentient. Insentient objects are transient and illusive. Ātman, which is Pure Sentience cannot be made up of the three Guṇas. A seeker can refute or discard the manifestations of the three Guṇas in meditation. However, eternal Ātman cannot be refuted or invalidated. Guṇas have their own characteristic properties. Ātman has no attributes, properties or characteristics. Guṇas bind the seeker (Bhagvad-Gītā 14.6). Ātman is never bounded or attached.

## Delusion of Jīva about his real Self

**यद्वन्मृदि घटभ्रान्तिं शुक्तौ वा रजतस्थितिम् ।**
**तद्वद्ब्रह्मणि जीवत्वं भ्रान्त्या पश्यति न स्वतः ॥ ५९ ॥**

*Yadvanmṛdi ghaṭabhrāntiṁ śuktou vā rajatasthitim /*
*Tadvadbrahmaṇi Jīvatvaṁ bhrāntyā paśyati na swataḥ // 59 //*

**यथा मृदि घटो नाम कनके कुण्डलाभिधा ।**
**शुक्तौ हि रजतख्यातिर्जीवशब्दस्तथा परे ॥ ६० ॥**

*Yathā mṛdi ghaṭo nāma kanake kuṇḍālābhidhā /*
*Śuktau hi rajatakhyātirjīvaśabdastathā pare // 60 //*

**Meaning:** A deluded person sees a pot in the place of clay, or silver in the place of sea-shell. Similarly, Jīva is seen in the place of Brahman. However, when one realizes Brahman as his Self, all delusions are eradicated. In deluded state, the clay is called by the name of a pot, gold is called by the name of an ornament and a sea-shell is known by the name of silver, and similarly Brahman is called by the name of a Jīva (individual soul).

These examples are very commonly used in Vedānta scriptures. They have sustained over hundreds of years, since they very aptly illustrate the fundamental principles of Vedānta.

| Object | Material Cause | Instrumental Cause |
|---|---|---|
| Pot | Earth | Potter |
| Ornament | Gold | Goldsmith |
| Silver | Seashell | Sunlight |

In these examples, the 'material cause' and the 'instrumental cause' are separate.

A pot may be red, black or white in color depending on the clay. However, the clay is only clay irrespective of any color it has. There may be many sizes, shapes and uses of pots, however, they are nothing but clay in essence. A pot is an illusion (Mithyā, मिथ्या) while clay is real (Satya, सत्य). Similarly, one needs to learn that Jīva (individual Consciousness) is an illusion and Brahman (universal, Pure Consciousness) is real. There may be more or less space inside the pot depending on its size and capacity. However, when a pot is broken, its space does not get added to the original big space, since the space inside the pot is not separate from the original big space in reality. All pots are created and destroyed in the same, vast original space. The space does not enter in the pot or exit from the pot. Similarly, Brahman does not enter in Jīva or leave the Jīva or exit from it. Brahman is everywhere. It is immovable, stable and constant. Hence, a pot is called as an Upādhi (limiting adjunct) of the space and the body is an Upādhi of Brahman. The existence of the space is not dependent on the pot. Similarly, the existence of Brahman is not dependent on the body (Jīva). Brahman is Absoute, all-pervasive, and ever-existent irrespective of anything else.

Jīva is falsely attributed on Brahman. Even though Brahman is vast, all-pervasive and expansive, it pervades the intellect in a specific and indirect manner. The intellect is made up of Sattvaguṇa and TejaTattva (fire element). The intellect is originally clear like a crystal, the light of Pure Consciousness (Ātman) can permeate it and reflect in it. The reflected light of Ātman in the intellect is called as Cidābhāsa (Reflected Consciousness). Cidābhāsa activates the intellect and all subtle desires (Vāsanās) in the intellect. This is the very reason why Jīva goes through birth-death cycle and gets his present body and birth. In deep-sleep, Reflected Consciousness i.e. Cidābhāsa becomes one with Pure Consciousness, since there is no intellect in the deep sleep. Cidābhāsa disappears in its original nature, Brahman. Hence Cidābhāsa is not eternal or real. One has to learn from Sadguru that the original nature of Jīva is not Cidābhāsa. Jīva is Brahman (Pure Consciousness) and nothing else. After Self-realization, Jīva himself says:

अहं ब्रह्मास्मि ।

*Aham Brahmāsmi* /

- I am Brahman.

Cidābhāsa and Brahman are one with each other just like a golden ornament is one with the gold. Everything else is an illusion. Ātman is light (Vastu, वस्तू), while Jīva is its radiance (Prabha, प्रभा). Ātman is gold and Jīva is an ornament. Jiva needs intellect, Prāṇa, body etc. to come into being as Jīva. Jīva also needs the elements in the world like food, water, air etc. for its sustenance. This system is established only to explain the illusive appearance of the world. From the perspective of Vedānta, only One Brahman (gold) is real. Manifold appearance of the world is as illusive as ornaments. The theory of Cidvilasavāda (चिद्विलासवाद) states the same thoery. Māyāvāda, states that Adhyāsta (falsely superimposed entity, अध्यस्त) cannot exist without its substratum (Adhiṣṭhāna, अधिष्ठान). Hence every falsely attributed object is only Brahman.

Māṇḍūkya Kārikā says -

**मायामात्रं इदं द्वैतं अद्वैतं परमार्थतः ।**

*Māyāmātraṁ idaṁ dvaitaṁ advaitaṁ Paramārthataḥ / (1.17)*

- 'Duality is incorrectly perceived only due to the presence of the illusive mind. In reality, only Advaita (non-duality) exists.'

Even though the mind perceives duality in the form of ornaments, in reality there is only one gold. Even though mind perceives 'falsely superimposed' (Adhyāsta) objects in the world, in reality there is only one Brahman. Gold is seen in the form of ornaments because of explicit modification (Anāvṛta Vivarta, अनावृत विवर्त). Snake is seen in the place of rope because of implicit modification (Āvṛta Vivarta, आवृत विवर्त) [Ācārya Bapat Shastri]. St. Gulabrao Mahārāja has stated these differences as Anadhyāsta Vivarta (अनध्यस्त विवर्त) and Adhyāsta Vivarta (अध्यस्त विवर्त) respectively. We may say that any one of these explanations is in sync with Ādi Śaṅkarā's philosophy.

## Examples to illustrate that everything is Brahman

**यथैव व्योम्नि नीलत्वं यथा नीरं मरुस्थले ।**

**पुरुषत्वं यथा स्थाणौ तद्वद्विश्वं चिदात्मनि ॥ ६१ ॥**

*Yathaiva vyomni nīlatvaṁ yathā nīraṁ marusthale /*

*Puruṣatvaṁ yathā sthāṇou tadvadviśvaṁ Cidātmāni // 61 //*

**Meaning:** Sky is incorrectly perceived as blue, mirage is incorrectly perceived on the desert and a person is incorrectly perceived on the bare tree-trunk. Similarly, the world is incorrecty perceived (to exist) on Ātman (Chidākāśa, चिदाकाश).

The sky is perceived as blue due to a specific scientific property of the blue color, which is distinct from other colors. In a completely dry desert, one incorrectly sees vast expanse of water (mirage). In partial darkness, a bare tree-trunk is perceived as a thief or demon by a scared person. The water of the mirage cannot be consumed. The blue color of the sky cannot be used for painting. The demon on the tree-trunk disappears as soon as there is enough light on it. Similarly, the world is incorrectly perceived as real due to ignorance (Ajñāna, अज्ञान). The world or worldly entities cannot be used for experiencing eternal happiness.

However, the elements of the world such as scriptures, Vedānta, Sadguru, spiritual practices etc. are useful (despite being illusory) for Self-realization and experiencing eternal, Pure Bliss of Ātman. In the end, all spiritual tools and practices become inconsequential for an enlightened person.

## The delusive appearance of the world

यथैव शून्ये वेतालो गन्धर्वाणां पुरं यथा ।

यथाकाशे द्विचन्द्रत्वं तद्वत्सत्ये जगत्स्थितिः ॥ ६२ ॥

*Yathaiva sūnye vetālo gandharvāṇāṁ puraṁ yathā /*

*Yathākāśe dvicandratvaṁ tadvatsatye jagatsthitiḥ // 62 //*

**Meaning:** In the evening, a ghost is delusively seen in an empty space, a castle or a city is delusively seen in the air due to clouds (white formations), and two moons are delusively seen in the sky. Similarly, the world is delusively seen in Brahman.

At dusk, one feels scared in a deserted place by imagining a ghost in the semi-dark space. White clouds come together to create many different fomations, such as palaces, or attaractive mansions in the sky. A person who is suffering from diplopia delusively sees two moons in the sky instead of one. In reality, there is no ghost in empty space, the cloud formations are imaginary, and two moons are seen only due to the defect in the eyes. These illusions disappear when there is enough light in the space, clouds fly away due to the wind and the eyes are corrected of the defect. Similarly, the world does not exist in Brahman.

When the taints on the intellect such as 'I am body' illusion or 'the world is real' illusion are eradicated, one experiences Brahman alone as the reality behind the illusive appearance of the world.

## Brahman appears as the world

यथा तरङ्गकल्लोलैर्जलमेव स्फुरत्यलम् ।
पात्ररूपेण ताम्रं हि ब्रह्माण्डौघैस्तथाऽऽत्मता ॥ ६३ ॥

*Yathā taraṅgakallolairjalameva sphuratyalam /*
*Pātrarūpenatāmraṁ hi Brahmānḍoughaistathā'tmatā // 63 //*

घटनाम्ना यथा पृथ्वी पटनाम्ना हि तन्तवः ।
जगन्नाम्ना चिदाभाति ज्ञेयं तत्तदभावतः ॥ ६४ ॥

*Ghaṭanāmnā yathā pṛthvi paṭanāmnā hi tantavaḥ /*
*Jagnnāmna Cidābhāti jñeyam tattadabhāvataḥ // 64 //*

**Meaning:** Water manifests in the form of ripples. Many vessels may be created from the metal of copper, but all of them contain only copper and nothing else. The clay manifests in the form of pots and threads appear in the form of cloth. Similarly, Pure Consciousness (Brahman) appears in the form of the world. All that is seen depends on the specific perspective.

Ripples in water are created by the wind. Copper vessels are created by a brazier, earthern pots are created by a potter, and clothes are created by a knitter. Thus, wind, potter, brazier and smith are called as 'extra creators' (Avāntar kāraṇa, अवांतर कारण) of their respective creations. There is also a perceiver, who sees ripples, vessels, pots, clothes as separate objects. In the example of ripples, the wind is a creator, water is material, and there is a separate knower (Pramātā, प्रमाता), who knows the wind and the water. Other examples have different creators, materials and knowers as well.

One can clearly understand that, in case of Brahman (appearing as the world), it is necessary to consider Īśvara (Brahman) as 'instrumental cause' unified with 'material cause' (AbhinnaNimittaUpādānaKāraṇa, अभिन्ननिमित्तउपादान-कारण) of the world. Examples evidently have their own limitations.

## All actions on the substratum of Pure Knowledge

सर्वोऽपि व्यवहारस्तु ब्रह्मणा क्रियते जनैः ।
अज्ञानान्न विजानन्ति मृदेव हि घटादिकम् ॥ ६५ ॥

*Sarvo'pi vyavahārastu Brahmanā kriyate janaiḥ /*
*Ajñānanna vijānanti mṛdeva hi ghatādikam // 65 //*

**Meaning:** People perform all activities on the substratum of Pure Knowledge of Brahman. All pots are of the nature of the clay; however, they are not known in that manner. Similarly, the fact that the world is of the nature of Brahman is not known. Pots are used even when their real nature is not known, similarly all worldly activities continue without knowing that they take place in Brahman.

The composition of this verse is somewhat mysterious. Hence, it is necessary to accept its explanation just like the one in Brahmasūtras.

All activities in day-to-day life are based in knowledge. Objects, memories, place, time, logic, experiments, guidance, laws of nature, life-death cycle, millions of species, good-bad or right-wrong discrimination etc. take place only with the help of knowledge. Brahman (Cit, चित्) is Pure Knowledge. It is the substratum of all activities. Reflected Consciousness (Cidābhāsa, चिदाभास) is the main tool for executing actions, since it activates the mind, and the mind becomes sentient for all practical purposes. Ignorant people do not understand that knowledge, organs Prāṇas, and objects are all necessary to lead the worldly life. It is easy to understand the generic knowledge gained by the intellect. However, not many people can pay attention to the Reflected Consciousness (Cidābhāsa, चिदाभास), which is present in the intellect; and its origin, Pure Consciousness, which is the substratum of all worldly knowledge. The transactional life can continue without the Knowledge of Brahman, however, one who seeks liberation must pursue it to the end. Brahman is the reality behind all appearances. Realizing that 'I am Brahman' is the main objective of spiritual science.

## The relation between the world and Brahman

कार्यकारणता नित्यमास्ते घटमृदोर्यथा ।
तथैव श्रुतियुक्तिभ्यां प्रपञ्चब्रह्मणोरिह ॥ ६६ ॥

*Kāryakāraṇatā nityamāste ghaṭamṛdoryathā |*
*Tathaiva śrutiyuktibhyāṁ prapañcabrahmaṇoriha || 66 ||*

**Meaning:** There is a cause and effect relationship between clay and the pot, and similarly between Brahman and the world. This has been established by (Vedāntic) scriptures and logic.

One of the Brahmasūtra says -

**शास्त्रयोनित्वात् ।**

*Śāstrayonitvāt / (1.1.3)*

- One gains complete knowledge of Brahman (as the real Self) with adequate studies of scriptures.

The relationship between Brahman and the visible world (Dṛśya) is included in this knowledge. Brahman is the cause and the world is its effect. This relationship is not the same as the one between germs and disease. It is also not the same as the one between the clay and a pot, or milk and curd. The clay is converted into a pot. Milk is converted into curd as per the theory of Parinamavāda (परिणामवाद). The relationship between Brahman and the world is the same as that of water and ice, where water is converted into ice without loosing its nature of water.

Brahmasūtra says -

**जन्माद्यस्य यतः ।**

Janmādyasya yataḥ / *(1.1.2)*

- (Ātman is that) from which the origin, sustenance and dissolution of this (world derive).

The commentary of Brahmasūtra states -

**यतो वा इमानि भूतानि जायन्ते ।**

*Yato vā imāni bhūtāni jāyante / (Tai. Up. 3.1.1)*

- That from which these beings are born (is Brahman).

Bṛhadāraṇyaka Upaniṣad says -

आत्मा अरे वा श्रोतव्यो मन्तव्यो ।

*Ātma are va śrotavyo mantavyo | (2.4.5)*

- One should hear only about Ātman and contemplate only on Ātman.

With the help of these Śrutis, one should reflect logically on the relationship between Brahman and world.

Just as the clay (cause) has entered into the pot (effect), Brahman (cause) has entered into the world (effect). Brahman itself has manifested in the form of the phenomenal world.

Upaniṣad states the same principle -

सर्वं खल्विदं ब्रह्म ।

*Sarvaṁ khalvidaṁ Brahman | (Chan. Up. 3.14.1)*

- In reality, everything is Brahman.

Ādi Śaṅkarācārya accepts and agrees with the theory of SarvaBrahmaVāda. Māyāvāda is another system, which states that Brahman as the substratum (Adhiṣṭhāna) is the cause, while the falsely superimposed (Adhyasta) world is its effect. The superimposed (world) does not have autonomous existence. It is ultimately of the nature of its substratum Brahman.

Both these theories (Sarvabrahmavāda and Māyāvāda) mention the same underlying principle in different words.

## The world is Brahman for an Enlightened Person

गृह्यमाणे घटे यद्वन्मृत्तिकाऽऽभाति वै बलात् ।
वीक्ष्यमाणे प्रपञ्चेऽपि ब्रह्मैवाभाति भासुरम् ॥ ६७ ॥

*Gṛhyamāṇe ghāṭe yadvanmṛttikā'bhāti vai balāt /*
*Vīkṣyamāṇe prapañce'pi Brahmaivābhāti bhāsuram // 67 //*

**Meaning:** While seeing the pot, one invariably sees the clay. Similarly, with subtle, deep thinking, one invariably sees the world as Self-effulgent Brahman.

St. Jñāneśwara says that the ignorant people perceive the world as real. This incorrect perception is the biggest obstacle in knowing Brahman. It is easy to see the clay in a pot. However, it is enormously difficult to see Brahman in the world. The world is made up of Aṣṭadha Prakṛti (अष्टधा प्रकृती, five great elements and three Guṇas). In this ever-changing dynamic world, Brahman is the only constant unchanging principle. In order to consistently think and remember this fact, the seeker needs subtle and Sattivic intellect, courage, patience, detachment and grace of Sadguru. One who is emotionally involved in routine worldly activities cannot contemplate on the underlying principle of Brahman. An ordinary person is engrossed in the world, a seeker is engrossed in spiritual practice, while an enlightened person rejoices in Ātman (आत्मक्रीड-Ātmakrīḍa, Muṇḍaka. Up. 3.1.4). After Self-realization, the enlightened person executes all external actions normally, while being connected to Ātman internally.

## Before and after Self-realization

सदैवात्मा विशुद्धोऽपि ह्यशुद्धो भाति वै सदा ।
यथैव द्विविधा रज्जुर्ज्ञानिनोऽज्ञानिनो निशम् ॥ ६८ ॥

*Sadaivātmā viśuddho'pi hyaśuddho bhāti vai sadā |*
*Yathaiva dvividhā rajjurjñānino'jñānino niśam || 68 ||*

**Meaning:** A rope is only one. In ignorance, it is delusively perceived as a snake and after knowledge it is seen as the rope. Similarly, Brahman is One. In ignorance it is perceived as the world, and after Self-realization, it is seen as Brahman.

A rope is always a rope, even if it is in a convoluted shape. One who delusively sees it as a snake gets scared by it, while one who sees it as a rope remains fearless. Bṛhadāraṇyaka Upaniṣad says -

द्वितीयाद्वै भयं भवति ।

*Dvitiyad vai bhayam bhavati | (1.4.2)*

- Where there is a second, there is fear.

In delusion, one object is mistakenly seen as a different object, which means there is duality. The main reason for fear is the appearance of duality in the world. Fear is a reflex action that is necessary for self-protection and survival. The body, wealth, family, prestige etc. need protection. One should perform prescribed duties meticulously towards his family, job etc. and then accept the results peacefully, as per the system of Īśvara. This builds fortitude (Titikṣā, तितिक्षा) in the seeker. According to Vedānta, the world is an illusive and unreal appearance.

Even then, it is extremely difficult to accept it in that manner. Hence, one should seek the help of Īśvara and surrender to Īśvara.

## Differentiation between Ātman and Anātmān

यथैव मृण्मयः कुंभस्तद्वद्देहोऽपि चिन्मयः ।
आत्मानात्मविभागोऽयं मुधैव क्रियतेऽबुधैः ॥ ६९ ॥

*Yathaiva mṛnmayaḥ kumbhastadvaddeho'pi cinmayaḥ |*
*Ātmānātmavibhāgo'yam mudhaiva kriyate'budhaiḥ || 69 ||*

**Meaning**: A pot is of the nature of the clay. Likewise, the body (world) is of the nature of Ātman. The division between Ātman and Anātmān is mistakenly done by ignorant people.

Here we should consider the word Adhyāropa (false attribution). Ādi Śaṅkarā says -

अध्यारोप अपवादाभ्यां निष्प्रपञ्चं प्रपञ्च्यते ।

*Adhyāropa apavādabhyāṃ niṣprapañcaṃ prapañcyate |*

- Adhyāropa is the initial, temporary acceptance of the existence of the world.

In a composition named Anātmāśrivigarhanam, Ādi Śaṅkarācārya specifically criticizes all that is unreal (Anātmān). On the other hand, he also promotes the fact that 'everything is verily Brahman' in his composition Ātmabodha.

1. In fact, the word 'everything' has no significance, since Ātman is only One reality.

2. But every entity in the visible world (Dṛśya, दृश्य) influences the human mind. Hence, it is necessary to speak about unreal objects in terms of 'all, every' etc.

The first statement above is purely meant to explain the theory of Vedānta, while the second statement is meant to help the seekers.

The non-duality of Ātman is explained in different ways by different theories. The theory of Ajātavāda propounds that the world is never born. Objects or people never come into being. However, Ajātavāda is discussed only by assuming the concept of birth. In the theory of Māyāvāda, one has to temporarily assume the existence of Māyic Adhyāsta (अध्यस्त, superimposed entities) and Adhiśthāna (अधिष्ठान, substratum) separately from each other. The treatise of Amṛtanubhāva (अमृतानुभव) explains the concept of Cit (चित्) and its manifestations by initially assuming them to be separate from each other.

One should understand and accept any of the above theories and get rid of the ignorance that Ātman is separate from Anātman (the world).

## Examples of identification with the body

**सर्पत्वेन यथा रज्जू रजतत्वेन शुक्तिका ।**

**विनिर्णीता विमूढेन देहत्वेन तथात्मता ॥ ७० ॥**

*Sarpatvena yathā rajjūrajatatvena śuktikā /*

*Vinirṇītā vimūḍhena dehatvena tathātmatā // 70 //*

**Meaning:** A rope is mistakenly seen as a snake and a shining sea-shell is mistaken for silver. Similarly, ignorant people deterministically call body as Ātman.

Vivarta (विवर्त) is an imaginary change, where an object is seen as something different due to delusion. Ātman is manifested as a body due to Vivarta. A rope is manifested in the form of a snake and and a shining sea-shell is manifested in the form of silver. The clay is manifested as a pot. Most people tend to remain engrossed in pots and ignore the clay. Human thoughts are centered on the size, shape, color, price, owner, utility, capacity of the pot. Similarly, people commonly think about color, height (body); propsperity, poverty (circumstances); birth, death (life) etc. In this commotion of thoughts, the fundamental principle of Ātman is completely sidelined. An ignorant person thinks that 'I am body', while an enlightened person knows that 'I am Ātman' and leads his life as dictated by destiny (Prārabdha, प्रारब्ध).

## Ātman is real, the world is unreal

घटत्वेन यथा पृथ्वी पटत्वेनैव तन्तवः ।
विनिर्णीता विमूढेन देहत्वेन तथात्मता ॥ ७१ ॥

*Ghaṭatvena yathā pṛthvi paṭatvenaiva tantavaḥ /*
*Vinirṇītā vimūḍhena dehatvena tathātmatā // 71 //*

कनकं कुण्डलत्वेन तरङ्गत्वेन वै जलम् ।
विनिर्णीता विमूढेन देहत्वेन तथात्मता ॥ ७२ ॥

*Kanakaṁ kuṇḍalatvena taraṅgatvena vai jalam /*
*Vinirṇītā vimūḍhena dehatvena tathātmatā // 72 //*

पुरुषत्वेन वै स्थाणुर्जलत्वेन मरीचिका ।
विनिर्णीता विमूढेन देहत्वेन तथात्मता ॥ ७३ ॥

*Puruṣatvena vai sthāṇurjalatvena marīcikā /*
*Vinirṇītā vimūḍhena dehatvena tathātmatā // 73 //*

गृहत्वेनैव काष्ठानि खड्गत्वेनैव लोहता ।
विनिर्णीता विमूढेन देहत्वेन तथात्मता ॥ ७४ ॥

*Grahatvenaiva kāṣṭāni, khaḍgtvenaiva lohatā /*
*Vinirṇītā vimūḍhena dehatvena tathātmatā // 74 //*

**Meaning:** The clay is surely seen as a pot, threads are seen as a cloth, gold is seen as an ornament, water is seen as ripple, bare tree-trunk is seen as a person, mirage is seen as real water, wood is seen as a house and iron is seen as a sword (in illusion). Similarly, Ātman is seen as a body (as a result of illusion).

All these examples are of the same kind and their meanings are evident. They are used only to strengthen the main principle that Ātman is real, while the world is unreal or just an illusive appearance.

## The body is seen as a result of ignorance

यथा वृक्षविपर्यासो जलाद्भवति कस्यचित् ।
तद्वदात्मनि देहत्वं पश्यत्यज्ञानयोगतः ॥ ७५ ॥

*Yathā vṛkṣaviparyāso jalādbhāvati kasyacit /*
*Tadvdātmani dehatvaṁ paśyatyajñānayogataḥ // 75 //*

पोतेन गच्छतः पुंसः सर्वं भातीव चञ्चलम् ।
तद्वदात्मनि देहत्वं पश्यत्यज्ञानयोगतः ॥ ७६ ॥

*Potena gaccataḥ puṁsaḥ sarvaṁ bhātīva cañcalam /*

*Tadvdātmani dehatvaṁ paśyatyajñānayogataḥ || 76 ||*

पीतत्वं हि यथा शुभ्रे दोषाद्भवति कस्यचित् ।
तद्वदात्मनि देहत्वं पश्यत्यज्ञानयोगतः ॥ ७७ ॥

*Pītatvaṁ hi yathā śubhre doṣādbhāvati kasyacit |*
*Tadvdātmani dehatvaṁ paśyatyajñānayogataḥ || 77 ||*

चक्षुर्भ्यां भ्रमशीलाभ्यां सर्वं भाति भ्रमात्मकम् ।
तद्वदात्मनि देहत्वं पश्यत्यज्ञानयोगतः ॥ ७८ ॥

*Cakṣurbhyāṁ bhramaśīlābhyāṁ sarvaṁ bhāti bhramātmākam |*
*Tadvdātmani dehatvaṁ paśyatyajñānayogataḥ || 78 ||*

**Meaning:** The reflection of a tree in water is mistaken for the real tree. A person who is travelling in a boat delusively sees everything around him in motion. One who is suffering from jaundice sees everything as yellow in color. A person suffering from vertigo sees everything whirling around him. Similar to all these examples, one sees body on account of ignorance. In reality, Pure Consciousness (Ātman) is the real Self.

## An example of alata (torch) in Māṇḍūkya Kārikā

अलातं भ्रमणेनैव वर्तुलं भाति सूर्यवत् ।
तद्वदात्मनि देहत्वं पश्यत्यज्ञानयोगतः ॥ ७९ ॥

*Aalātaṁ bhramaṇenaiva vartulaṁ bhāti sūryavat |*
*Tadvdātmani dehatvaṁ paśyatyajñānayogataḥ || 79 ||*

**Meaning**: When a burning torch is moved speedily in circular motion, it looks like a round, bright sun. Similarly, Ātman is perceived as a body on account of ignorance.

The body, the mind, human life and the world undergo continuous movement and change. Because of their dynamic motion, one cannot experience the static principle of Brahman, which is their substratum. To minimize the dynamic motion (of body, mind etc.) and keep it under control is known as detachment. An enlightened person, who may not be a formal monk, can be seen working dynamically from outside. However, internally he has realized Oneness with the static, unchanging, constant principle of Brahman. In formal renunciation, however, one must necessarily control all dynamic worldly actions. Otherwise, the whole renunciation becomes meaningless.

## Examples of ignorance

**महत्त्वे सर्ववस्तूनामणुत्वं ह्यतिदूरतः ।**
**तद्वदात्मनि देहत्वं पश्यत्यज्ञानयोगतः ॥ ८० ॥**

*Mahatve sarvavastūnāmaṇutvam hyatidūrataḥ /*
*Tadvdātmani dehatvaṁ paśyatyajñānayogataḥ // 80 //*

**सूक्ष्मत्वे सर्ववस्तूनां स्थूलत्वं चोपनेत्रतः ।**
**तद्वदात्मनि देहत्वं पश्यत्यज्ञानयोगतः ॥ ८१ ॥**

*Sūkṣmatve sarvavastūnāṁ sthūlatvaṁ copanetrataḥ /*
*Tadvdātmani dehatvaṁ paśyatyajñānayogataḥ // 81 //*

**काचभूमौ जलत्वं वा जलभूमौ हि काचता ।**
**तद्वदात्मनि देहत्वं पश्यत्यज्ञानयोगतः ॥ ८२ ॥**

*Kācabhūmou jalatvam va jalabhūmou hi kācatā /*
*Tadvdātmani dehatvaṁ paśyatyajñānayogataḥ // 82 //*

**यद्वदग्नौ मणित्वं हि मणौ वा वह्निता पुमान् ।**
**तद्वदात्मनि देहत्वं पश्यत्यज्ञानयोगतः ॥ ८३ ॥**

*Yadvadagnou maṇitvam hi maṇou vā vahnitā pumān /*

*Tadvdātmani dehatvaṁ paśyatyajñānayogataḥ // 83 //*

अभ्रेषु सत्सु धावत्सु धावन्निव यथा शशी ।

तद्वदात्मनि देहत्वं पश्यत्यज्ञानयोगतः ॥ ८४ ॥

*Abhreṣu satsu dhāvatsu dhāvanniva yathā śaśī /*

*Tadvdātmani dehatvaṁ paśyatyajñānayogataḥ // 84 //*

यथैव दिग्विपर्यासो मोहाद्भवति कस्यचित् ।

तद्वदात्मनि देहत्वं पश्यत्यज्ञानयोगतः ॥ ८५ ॥

*Yathaiva digviparyāso mohādbhāvati kasyacit /*

*Tadvdātmani dehatvaṁ paśyatyajñānayogataḥ // 85 //*

यथा शशी जले भाति चञ्चलत्वेन कस्यचित् ।

तद्वदात्मनि देहत्वं पश्यत्यज्ञानयोगतः ॥ ८६ ॥

*Yathā śaśī jale bhāti cañcalatvena kasyacit /*

*Tadvdātmani dehatvaṁ paśyatyajñānayogataḥ // 86 //*

**Meaning:** A giant object looks small from distance (e.g. the sun). A tiny object looks big through an instrument such as microscope. On a vast clear-glass platform, there is an illusion of water (e.g. Mayasabhā in Mahabhārata), or in a clear-water lake, there is an illusion of glass. There is an illusion of fire in a resplendent jewel, or there is an illusion of a jewel in a soft blue light. Occassionally, when clouds float around the moon, it appears as if the moon itself is running. Sometimes one goes in a wrong direction due to delusion. The reflection of moon in water looks as if its shievering when there are ripples in water. Just like these examples, Ātman (the real Self) is mistaken to be the body on account of ignorance.

These examples explain different kinds and experiences of illusions. In the same manner, walking, speaking, executing actions, experiencing joy and grief, diseases, birth and death are all pertinent to the body (gross, subtle and causal). Ātman is completely detached from them, yet all experiences and actions are superimposed on Ātman. E.g. I am sick, I am sad, I am walking etc. Ātman pervades the body yet stays completely detached from it. No action executed by the body can touch Ātman in any manner. Identification of the Self with the body is called Dehadhyāsa (देहाध्यास) or Dehabuddhi (देहबुद्धी) or Dehatādātmya (देहतादात्म्य).

## Eradicating the illusion that 'I am body'

**एवमात्मन्यविद्यातो देहाध्यासो हि जायते ।**
**स एवात्मपरिज्ञानाल्लीयते च परात्मनि ॥ ८७ ॥**
*Evamātmanyavidyāto dehādhyāso hi jāyate |*
*Sa evātmaparijñānallīyate ca parātmani || 87 ||*

**Meaning:** This is how, body is superimposed on the real Self (Svarūpa) because of ignorance. After Self-realization (I am Ātman), the illusion that 'I am body' disappears in Ātman, the real Self.

The snake disappears in the rope, the silver disappears in the shining sea-shell and the thief disappears in the bare tree-trunk after knowing the reality in these cases. Similarly, after Self-realization, the illusion that 'I am body' disappears in Brahman. Due to the incorrect notion that 'I am the body, mind, intellect or ego'; the characteristics of body, mind etc. are falsely superimposed on Ātman, the real 'I'. The ignorance that leads to Adhyāsa disappears in Ātman along with Adhyāsa.

The false superimposition of the body on the real Self, and the real Self on the body is called as Anyonyadhyāsa (अन्योन्याध्यास, mutual superimposition), which is eradicated after Self-realization. This process is also known as Jīva-Brahmaikya, Ātmajñāna, Ātmabrahmaikya, Mokṣa, Paramapada Prāpti, Naiṣakarmyasiddhi etc. It is as if one re-attains what is ever-attained (Nityaprāpta, नित्यप्राप्त).

## All worldly entities are Ātman

सर्वमात्मतया ज्ञातं जगत्स्थावरजङ्गमम् ।
अभावात्सर्वभावानां देहानां चात्मता कुतः ॥ ८८ ॥

*Sarvamātmatayā jñātaṁ jagatsthāvarajaṅgamam /*
*Aabhāvātsarvabhāvānāṁ dehanāṁ cātmatā kutaḥ // 88 //*

**Meaning:** All stationary and moving objects are verily seen as Ātman. All of these objects are transient. So how can the body be real or eternal?

Upaniṣad says -

सर्वं खल्विदं ब्रह्म ।

*Sarvaṁ khalvidaṁ Brahman / (Chān. Up. 3.14.1)*

- In reality, everything is Brahman.

केन कं पश्येत् ।

*Kena kaṁ pashyet / (Bru. Up. 4.5.15)*

- (When everything is Brahman) who will see whom (separately)?

The resultant experience of these Śrutis is mentioned in this verse. Both Śrutis together state that when everything is verily Brahman, there is no separation between perceiver and perceived, or knower and known (Pramātā and Prameya). With complete assimilation and culmination of this knowledge after Self-realization, the (enlightened) person experiences BādhaSamādhi (sublation of the world in the mind while executing all actions).

Dṛk Dṛśya Viveka says -

**यत्र यत्र मनो याति तत्र तत्र समाधयः ।**

*Yatra yatra mano yati tatra tatra samadhayaḥ / (30)*

- [One who has dissociated from the attachment to the body and realized that 'I am Ātman'] experiences (uninterrupted) Samādhi wherever his mind goes.

## The ideal way to live life

**आत्मानं सततं जानन्कालं नय महामते ।**

**प्रारब्धमखिलं भुञ्जन्नोद्वेगं कर्तुमर्हसि ॥ ८९ ॥**

*Ātmānaṁ satataṁ jānankalaṁ naya mahāmate /*

*Prārabdham akhilaṁ bhuñjanodvegaṁ kartumarhasi //89 //*

**Meaning:** O intelligent one! Spend your life as per Prārabdha (destiny) while always remaining soaked in Ātman. Don't feel distressed.

This remark is meant for seekers. It indicates the ideal way to spend life as an enlightened person. When one consistently thinks and discriminates between Ātman and Anātmān (real and unreal), all unreal entities eventually take a back-seat. Mind gradually becomes stable in Ātman, the real Self. (Material) life is bound to proceed as per the system of Prārabdha. Many joyful or distressful incidents may happen in life; however, it is not mandatory for a seeker to become happy or unhappy with changing circumstances around him. St. Jñāneśwara states in his treatise that one should stay equipoised in both joyful and distressful circumstances, and not get carried away in the wake of events. Once the mind is established in equipoise, one may say that the seeker has attained enlightenment. This is a way to verify one's progress.

St. Jñāneśwara says that one should not pay attention to the characteristics of the gross body or the subtle body and meditate on the fact that 'I am Brahman'. He should consistently practice absorbing the Pure Bliss of Brahman. Distressed seeker or devotee is a paradoxical language in spiritual pursuit.

## No effect of Prārabdha after steady Self-realization

उत्पन्नेऽप्यात्मविज्ञाने प्रारब्धं नैव मुञ्चति ।
इति यच्छ्रूयते शास्त्रे तन्निराक्रियतेऽधुना ॥ ९० ॥

*Uthpanne'pyātmavijñāne prārabdham naiva muñcati /*
*Iti yatchruyate sāstre tannirākriyate'dhunā // 90 //*

**Meaning:** Scriptures describe the theory that Prārabdha continues to yield its effect even after Self-realization. This theory is being verified (and refuted) here (in this verse).

There are three kinds of actions in human life -

- **Sa□ciṭa Karma** (संचित कर्म): Accumulated actions of a Jīva (embodied soul) from all past human births. Jīva has to endure results of all actions (good or bad) at some point in time. Only after Self-realization, these accumulated actions are completely eradicated.
- **Prārabdha Karma** (प्रारब्ध कर्म): Fructescent actions from Sañciṭa Karma, on account of which Jīva gets his body in the current birth. The body lasts so long as these actions continue to produce their results.
- **Kriyamāṇa Karma** (क्रियमाण कर्म): Fresh new actions performed by Jīva. If new actions are done with 'I am the doer' mindset and in a selfish manner, they get added to the Sañciṭa of that Jīva.

Sañciṭa and Prārabdha continue to yield their effect on the body. Joy and grief are experienced because of events dictated by Prārabdha. Scriptures state that after the ultimate Knowledge of Brahman, all accumulated actions (Sañciṭa) from past births are turned into ashes, which means they stop being fruitive and do not produce any result. Fresh new actions (Kriyamāṇa karma) are not binding since they are executed with a non-doer mindset in selfless manner. Prārabdha continues to yield its effect for current birth and ends after fully living through its effects.

However, the reality of all enlightened saints is explained by St. Tukārāma in this verse (Tu. Ga 1229)

**संचित प्रारब्ध क्रियमाण । अवघा झाला नारायण ।**

*Sañcita Prārabdha Kriyamāṇa / Avhaghā jhālā Nārāyaṇa /*

- All (my) actions (and their results) are now just the form of Narayaṇa (Īśvara or the God).

Thus, a Self-realized person does not experience joy or grief like ordinary people. Prārabdha creates good or bad situations even in the life of a Self-realized person. However, he does not become happy or sad with changing circumstances around him. Ego, mind, organs and the visible world (Dṛśya, दृश्य) are sublated for all enlightened people. Hence their Kriyamāṇa Karma does not produce any new results.

Muṇḍaka Upaniṣad says -

स विद्वान्पुण्यपापे विधूय परमसाम्यमुपैति ।

*Sa vidvānpuṇyapāpe vidhūya paramasāmyamupaiti / (3.1.3)*

- A Self-realized sage performs day-to-day actions (Kriyamāṇa Karma) without any expectations. So, they do not produce any fruits or results. They are not binding for him. Prārabdha Karma comes to an end after fully living through its effects.

In Naiṣkarmyasiddhi, St. Sureśvarācārya says -

दग्धाखिलाधिकारश्चेत्ब्रह्म ज्ञानाग्निना मुनिः ।

वर्तमानः श्रुतेर्मूर्ध्नि नैव स्याद्वेदकिङ्करः ॥

*Dagdhākhilādhikāraścetabrahma jñānagninā muniḥ /*

*Vartamanaḥ śṛtermūrdhnir naiva syadvedakiṅkaraḥ // (1.40)*

- Kriyamāṇa karma are eradicated after the fire of Self-realization starts burning. Such enlightened saint need not follow the orders of Vedas, instead he shines as the jewel in crown of Vedas.

## Waking up from dream and ignorance are the same

तत्त्वज्ञानोदयादूर्ध्वं प्रारब्धं नैव विद्यते ।

देहादीनामसत्यत्वात् यथा स्वप्नः प्रबोधतः ॥ ९१ ॥

*Tattvajñānodayādūrdhvaṁ Prārabdhaṁ naiva vidyate /*

*Dehādīnāmasatyatvāt yathā swapnaḥ prabodhataḥ //91 //*

**Meaning:** A dream becomes inconsequential and unreal (Mithyā) after one wakes up from sleep. Similarly, the body and the world are seen as mere illusion after Self-realization, and Prārabdha verily ceases to exist.

Māyā is Aghaṭita-ghaṭanā-paṭiyasī (अघटित-घटना-पटियसी), which means it is adept at showing creations and incidences that are totally inconceivable. It creates the universe, which is neither real nor unreal hence indescribable (Sat-Asat-Vilakshana-Anirvacaniya).

It is difficult to first accept this thoery, believe in it, be firmly established in the knowledge, and later live naturally in the world knowing fully well that everything is transient (Māyā). This is the very gist of the path of Knowledge (Jñānayoga, ज्ञानयोग). The theory of Māyā is highly useful in the initial stages of spiritual pursuit. Knowing that everything is Māyā helps the seeker remain calm in good, bad or adverse situations. This Viveka eventually leads to detachment (Vairagya) and the worldly matters stop being troublesome. After Self-realization, the seeker experiences the state of sublation (Badha, बाध) as described in Dṛk Dṛśya Viveka -

यत्र यत्र मनो याति तत्र तत्र समाधयः ।

*Yatra yatra mano yati tatra tatra samadhayah / (30)*

- [One who has dissociated from the attachment to the body and realized that 'I am Ātman'] experiences (uninterrupted) Samādhi wherever his mind goes.

This stage is called as Bādha-Samādhi (A Samādhi where world is sublated in thoughts). All enlightened saints did enormous work for the society by leading life in this Samādhi. Prārabdha rules the body and the worldly life of enlightened sages as well. But, for them new Prārabdha is not created as a result of weakening of Vāsanās. Even then, Vāsanās, which are part of Prārabdha yield their influence on an enlightened person. Human life is extremely complex and intertwined with each other's life. Hence, the give-and-take transactions continue to take place for one and all. E.g. mother-son, father-daughter, husband-wife, brother-sister, friends, neighbors, coworkers etc. This complexity is comprehended by a very few discerning people. Hence, there are many misconceived notions about people in spiritual field.

## An enlightened person does not have Prārabdha

कर्म जन्मान्तरकृतं प्रारब्धमिति कीर्तितम् ।

तत्तु जन्मान्तराभावात्पुंसो नैवास्ति कर्हिचित् ॥ ९२ ॥

*Karma janmāntarakṛtam Prārabdhamiti kīrtitam /*

*Tattu janmāntarābhāvātpuṁso naivāsti karhicit // 92 //*

**Meaning:** Scriptures state that actions from the past birth create Prārabdha. However, an enlightened person does not have any future birth, so the concept of Prārabdha is moot in his case.

Sañciṭa Karma (संचित कर्म) is an accumulated result of all actions from past human births. Prārabdha Karma (प्रारब्ध कर्म) are the fructescent actions from Sañciṭa, on account of which, Jīva gets his body in the current birth [See verse 90]. Even for enlightened people, Prārabdha continues to yield their results. The blades of a moving fan keep rotating even after it is switched off. The day-to-day life of an enlightened person continues in the same manner, even after his accumulated past actions (Sañciṭa) are eradicated.

Bhagvad-Gītā says -

**ज्ञानाग्निः सर्व कर्माणि भस्मसात् कुरुते तथा ।**

*Jñānāgniḥ sarva karmāṇi bhasmasāt kurute tathā / (4-37)*

- After the ultimate Knowledge of Brahman, all accumulated actions (Sañciṭa) from past births are turned into ashes, i.e. they stop being fruitive and do not produce any result.

Even though Sañcita and Kriyamāṇa are eradicated, Prārabdha continues to have its effect. Enlightened sages who follow the path of devotion consider all actions (and their results) to be the form of Nārāyaṇa (Īśvara or the God), as explained in verse 90 in this commentary. They encounter both good or bad situations in life; however, they can remain equipoised in all situations due to unconditional surrender in Īśvara.

## Body in the waking same as the one in the dream

स्वप्नदेहो यथाध्यस्तस्तथैवायं हि देहकः ।

अध्यस्तस्य कुतो जन्म जन्माभावे स्थितिः कुतः ॥ ९३ ॥

*Swapnadeho yathādhyāstastathaivāyaṁ hi dehakaḥ /*

*Adhyāstasya kuto janma janmābhāve sthitiḥ kutaḥ //93 //*

**Meaning:** The body in the waking is superimposed (Adhyasta) just like the one in the dream state. If so, how could there be any birth of the (superimposed) body? If there is no birth, how can the body execute any action?

In the dream state, no body (self and others) has real existence. Similarly, in the waking state, when the incorrect thought that 'I am body' is eradicated, the body becomes inconsequential, just like a shadow. It remains just a puppet in the hands of Prārabdha. Hence, actions executed by the sublated (Bādhita, बाधित) Jīva in and through the sublated body do not yield any results. (After Self-realization), Sañcita karma is turned into ashes, Prārabdha comes to an end with the end of the body and Kriyamāṇa being executed by the body is inconsequential. In such a case, how can there be an emphasis on any action at all?

## Insignificance of the worldly life after Knowledge

उपादानं प्रपञ्चस्य मृद्भाण्डस्येव कथ्यते ।

अज्ञानं चैव वेदान्तैस्तस्मिन्नष्टे क्व विश्वता ॥ ९४ ॥

*Upādānam prapañcasya mṛdbhāṇḍasyeva kathyate /*

*Ajñānaṁ caiva Vedāntaistasminnaṣṭe kva viśvata //94 //*

**Meaning:** The clay is the 'material cause' of the pot. Similarly, ignorance (Ajñāna, अज्ञान) is the 'material cause' of the world. If ignorance is eradicated with the help of Knowledge, then how can the world have a real existance?

A pot with a name and a form is delusively seen in the clay. Similarly, the world with many names and forms is delusively seen in Brahman. This illusion is a result of ignorance.

It is imperative to accept that Brahman is AbhinnaNimittaUpādānaKāraṇa (अभिन्ननिमित्तउपादानकारण) i.e. both the 'instrumental cause' and 'material cause' of the universe. Otherwise, the theory of Kevala Advaita (Pure Non-Duality) does not sustain. The theory of ĪśvaraKāraṇavāda (ईश्वरकारणवाद) states that the entire world is created by Īśvara (the God). This theory has a wide-spread acceptance in masses. However, in Vedānta, Īśvara is ultimately Māyic (MāyāvishiṣṭaCetan, मायाविशिष्ट चेतन), hence the world created by Him should be considered Māyic (transient) as well. Once the world is accepted as an imaginary appearance, all objects, people, scriptures, actions can be seen in the same manner. Actions are transient, so their results (fruits) become naturally inconsequential. Alternatively, as per the theory of SarvaBrahmavāda (सर्वब्रह्मवाद), the entire world is verily Brahman, hence all actions are Brahman as well. All superimposed (Adhyāsta) entities have no autonomous existence without the substratum (Adhiṣṭhāna). Therefore, it is evident that irrespective of any theory, actions do not produce any results.

## The result of the delusive mind

**यथा रज्जुं परित्यज्य सर्पं गृह्णाति वै भ्रमात् ।**
**तद्वत्सत्यमविज्ञाय जगत्पश्यति मूढधीः ॥ ९५ ॥**

*Yathā rajjuṁ parityajya sarpaṁ gṛhṇāti vai bhramāt /*
*Tadvatsatyamavijñāya jagatpaśyati mūḍhadhiḥ // 95 //*

**Meaning:** Just as a person perceives only the snake instead of a rope, ignorant person perceives only the world (without knowing the reality behind it).

The word is transient, unreal and illusive (Mithyā, मिथ्या). However, once it is seen as real, it leads attachment to the worldly objects. One who forgets the fact that 'I am Pure Bliss (Brahman)', seeks happiness in material objects and other people. Most people think that more worldly objects lead to more happiness. This is the result of ignorance. Only the deep study of scriptures puts a stop to this futile thought-process and Jīva realizes that I am (Pure) Existence, Consciousness, Bliss i.e. (Sat, Cit, Ānanda) Brahman.

## Superimposition inconsequential after the Knowledge

**रज्जुरूपे परिज्ञाते सर्पभ्रान्तिर्न तिष्ठति ।**
**अधिष्ठाने तथा ज्ञाते प्रपञ्चः शून्यतां व्रजेत् ॥ ९६ ॥**

*Rajjurūpe parijñāte sarpabhrantirna tiṣṭati /*
*Adhiṣṭhane tatha jñāte prapañca śūnyatām vrajet // 96 //*

**Meaning:** The illusion that 'this is a snake' disappears with the knowledge that 'this is rope'. Similarly, the illusive appearance of the world disappears with the knowledge of Brahman.

One may interact with the world in different ways. However, when the worldly interactions are minimized, it is easy to sublate (Bādha) the world and make the superimposition (Adhyasta) of the world disappear in its substratum (Adhiṣṭhāna) Brahman. The world is made up of the quintuplicated (Pancikṛta, पंचीकृत) five great elements, which are insentient and Māyic in nature. The mind is made up from the wind element, the intellect is made up from the fire, and the ego is made up of the earth element. As per the theory of quintuplication, one can meditate in reverse order from earth-water-fire-wind-sky to Brahman. It is easy to meditate on the thought that the earth disappears in water, water disappears in fire and so on. Ultimately the sky disappears in Brahman. The sky is superimposed, while Brahman is its substratum. With the knowledge of Brahman, the superimposed world disappears in it. In other words, one stops seeing the world as real and sees Brahman alone as real.

## Generic rule for a Self-realized person and Prārabdha

देहस्यापि प्रपञ्चत्वात्प्रारब्धावस्थितिः कुतः ।
अज्ञानिजनबोधार्थं प्रारब्धं वक्ति वै श्रुतिः ॥ ९७ ॥

*Dehasyāpi prapañcatvatprārabdhāvasthitiḥ kutaḥ /*
*Ajñānijñābodhārthaṁ Prārabdhaṁ vakti vai śrutiḥ // 97 //*

**Meaning:** The body is ultimately a part of the world (which itself is a superimposition and a mere appearance). So, how can the (superimposed) body bear the effect of Prārabdha? However, only for understanding of ignorant people, Śruti states the generic rule that even enlightened people bear the effect of Prārabdha.

Wise people say that the Vedāntic scriptures should be taught with the following principle -

सर्वेषाम् अविरोधेन ।

*Sarveṣām Avirodhena* /

- In a manner that is not opposed by masses.

Millions of people are ignorant about the real Self from the spiritual perspective. Hence, they must be taught Vedānta in a way that is easily agreed, digested and accepted by them. St. Rāmadāsa says in his treatise Dāsabodha that the seeker should listen to everything, but thoughtfully accept only the real, meaningful gist and discard everything else. This verse explains the very gist of the theory of Vedānta. It contains guidance in the purest form. Even then, this guidance must be imparted in a way that is easily embraced by spiritually ignorant people. A child is taught step-by-step, gently in a way liked by him. The ordinary people need to be taught the theory of Vedānta in a similar manner. 'Enlightened people do not identify themselves with the body, so they do not bear the results of Prārabdha which is only effective at the level of the body'. If ignorant people listen to this guidance, they may only remember the part of 'no Prārabdha', which is disruptive for their own progress and spiritual pursuit.

## Śruti states that a Self-realized sage has no Prārabdha

क्षीयन्ते चास्य कर्माणि तस्मिन्दृष्टे परावरे ।
बहुत्वं तन्निषेधार्थं श्रुत्या गीतं च यत्स्फुटम् ॥ ९८ ॥
*Kṣīyante cāsya karmāṇi tasmin dṛṣte parāvare /*
*Bahutvam tanniśedhārtha śṛtyā gītaṁ ca yatsphutam // 98 //*

**Meaning:** All actions of a person are eradicated when he realizes the highest principle of Ātman as his Self. The word Karmāṇi (कर्माणि) indicates actions. (The verse indicates that) all actions including Sañcita are eradicated after Self-realization. Munḍaka Upaniṣad says -

भिद्यते हृदयग्रंथिः छिद्यन्ते सर्वसंशयाः ।
क्षीयन्ते चास्य कर्माणि तस्मिन् दृष्टे परावरे ॥
*Bhidyate hṛdayagranthiḥ chidyante sarvasañśayāḥ /*
*Kṣīyante cāsya karmāṇi tasmin dṛṣte parāvare // (2.2.8)*

- After Self-realization, all knots (bondages) of the heart (Antaḥkaraṇa) are broken, all doubts are resolved and all actions (and their results) wear away.

Brahman is Parāvara (परावर). The word Para indicates 'high' i.e. cause and Avara indicates 'low' i.e. effect (universe etc.). Brahman is all-pervasive and omnipresent, both in the cause and the effect. After realizing that 'I am Brahman', all knots of ignorance in the mind (Antaḥkaraṇa) are cut asunder. As a result, all actions wear away. 'All actions' include the three types of actions, which are Sañcita, Prārabdha, Kriyamāṇa.

The word Citjaḍagranthi (चिज्जडग्रंथी) indicates that the insentient body is considered as sentient, while sentient Ātman is considered as insentient. In reality, all insentient entities and sentient beings (Jīva) cannot exist without the Pure Consciousness of Ātman. Prārabdha is pertinent to the body (Jīva) and Jīva does not have a real existence. One who realizes the union of Jīva and Brahman (I am Brahman) does not consider himself as Jīva, hence he does not have to bear the results of Prārabdha. Māṇḍūkya Kārikā states the ultimate principle of Advaita in this verse-

**न कश्चिद् जायते जीवो संभवस्य न विद्यते ।**

*Na kaścid jāyate jīvo sambhāvasaya na vidyāte* /

- Jīva was never born, so he cannot possibly exist for real.

## An Enlightened Person has no Prārabdha

**उच्यतेऽज्ञैर्बलाच्चैतत्तदानर्थद्वयागमः ।**

**वेदान्तमतहानञ्च यतो ज्ञानमिति श्रुतिः ॥ ९९ ॥**

*Ucyate'jñairbalāccaitattadānarthadvayāgamaḥ* /

*Vedāntamatahānañca yato jñānamiti śṛtiḥ* // *99* //

**Meaning:** Even after all this (explanation), those who deliberately think that an enlightened person has Prārabdha, invite two big defects (blames) upon themselves -

1. Not accepting the knowledge of Śruti
2. Non-existence of the knowledge

If an enlightened person indeed has Prārabdha, then the whole concept of liberation becomes moot or irrelevant. This is against the knowledge propounded by Śruti. It refutes the theorem of Sañcita Karma expounded by Gītā verse 4.37 (See explanation of verse 92 in this text).

It also refutes the following verses in Upaniṣads

सा काष्ठा सा परागतिः ।

*Sā kaṣṭha sā parāgatiḥ | (Katha Up. 1.3.11)*

- Beyond the Puruṣa (Brahman), there is nothing. That is the highest limit. That is the highest goal.

क्षीयन्तेचास्यकर्माणि ।

*Kṣiyante cāsya karmāṇi | (Muṇḍ. Up. 2.2.8)*

- All actions perish (for a Self-realized person).

ब्रह्मवेद ब्रह्मैव भवति ।

*Brahaved Brahmaiva bhāvati | (Mund. Up. 3.2.9)*

- He who knows Brahman, becomes Brahman.

When the authentic verses of Śruti and Smṛti are refuted or invalidated, the entire spiritual pursuit becomes baseless and pointless.

Now, we will discuss the practice of Nididhyāsana (निदिध्यासन), which is truly essential for Self-realization - that is discussed so far in this treatise. The word Nididhyāsana means 'constant deep contemplation or meditation' of Ātman. Vedāntic scriptures consist of highly subtle, complex and profound theories. There are various approaches, opinions and interpretations of these texts. It is necessary to have extremely sharp and subtle intellect to comprehend these scriptures. One should be able to first get a general feel of the doctrine, then gain deep insight into it, and eventually develop firm grip on the philosophy. For this purpose, Ādi Śaṅkarācārya is now going to explain the practice of Nididhyāsana.

## Deep, steady contemplation (Nididhyāsana)

त्रिपञ्चाङ्गान्यतो वक्ष्ये पूर्वोक्तस्यैव सिद्धये ।
तैश्च सर्वैः सदा कार्यं निदिध्यासनमेव तु ॥ १०० ॥

*Tripañcaṅgānyato vakṣye pūrvoktasyaiva siddhaye /*
*Taiśca sarvaiḥ sadā kāryaṁ Nididhyāsanameva tu // 100 //*

**Meaning:** Now, for the realization of the theoretical knowledge explained so far, we will discuss fifteen specific aspects of Nididhyāsana.

आत्मा अरे वा श्रोतव्यो मन्तव्यो निदिध्यासितव्यः ।

*Ātmā are vā śrotavyo mantavyo nididhyāsitavyaḥ / (Bru.Up 4.5.6)*

- One should hear only about Ātman and contemplate, meditate only on Ātman.

The prescribed sequence for the study of Vedānta mentioned in the above verse is as follows -

- ***Śravana*** (श्रवण) - First, one should listen to the discourses of Vedāntic scriptures.
- ***Manana*** (मनन) - Listening should be coupled with intent deliberation, pondering on various aspects of the philosophy until all doubts are eradicated, and the fact that 'Jīva is Brahman' is fixed in mind.
- ***Nididhyāsana*** (निदिध्यासन) - Lastly, one should ingest the knowledge, contemplate and meditate deeply on the One principle of Brahman and assimilate it completely.

In day-to-day life, (verbal) engagements culminate into marriage. Similarly, *Soham* (सोऽहम्, I am that - Brahman) is a verbal commitment. It needs to culminate into actual Self-realization indicated by *Aham Brahmāsmi* (अहं ब्रह्मास्मि, I am Brahman). This journey starts only after attaining the Fourfold Preliminary Qualifications (Sādhana-Catuṣṭaya). St. Jñāneśwara states in his treatise Jñāneśwari (5.87) that one should resolutely meditate on Brahman. For this purpose, it is necessary to take the help of following specific fifteen aspects of Nididhyāsana. Brahmasūtra gives the same message -

**तन्निष्ठस्य मोक्षोपदेशात् ।**

*Tanniṣṭhasya Mokṣopadeśāt | (1.1.7)*

- One who keeps utmost faith in that [Ātman], attains liberation.

## **The necessity of nididhyāsana**

**नित्याभ्यासादृते प्राप्तिर्न भवेत्सच्चिदात्मनः ।**

**तस्माद्ब्रह्म निदिध्यासेज्जिज्ञासुः श्रेयसे चिरम् ॥ १०१ ॥**

*Nithyābhyāsādṛte prāptirna bhāvetsacidātmanaḥ |*

*Tasmādbrahma Nididhyāsejijñāsuḥ sreyase ciram || 101 ||*

**Meaning:** One cannot attain Aparokṣānubhūti (the direct Self-realization) of Brahman without consistent study and practice. Hence, a genuine yearner of Mokṣa (Mumukṣu) should constantly meditate upon Brahman for his highest benefit.

A seeker should have following qualifications -

- Strong desire of liberation (Mokṣa, मोक्ष)
- Systematic thinking on Brahman as guided by scriptures
- Firm resolve that the real epitome of human life is only in Aparokṣānubhūti of Brahman

Śruti propounds three step practices for the same purpose -

- Śravaṇa (श्रवण) - To get a good understanding and feel of Brahman.
- Manana (मनन) - To learn various peripheral theories and arguments both favoring and opposing Self-realization and make firm resolve that 'I am Brahman'.
- Nididhyāsana (निदिध्यासन) - The verbal resolve turns into firm, direct realization that 'I am Brahman', which later evolves into a steady, consistent experience.

Katha Upaniṣad says that the worldly life is Preya (प्रेय), and spiritual pursuit for Mokṣa is Śreya (श्रेय). Most people crave for Preya that gives transient happiness, while Śreya leads us towards the ultimate, Absolute, Pure Bliss that is not dependent upon other people or objects. Śreya indicates the supreme welfare of human life.

A seeker should deprioritize all worldly matters for spiritual pursuit and concentrate on the path of liberation (Śreya). All desires, hopes, ambitions, goals, achievables, ideas of meaningful human life, mountains of (unnecessary) social responsibilities, politics etc. need to be set aside to progress on the path of Self-realization. Human life is an intricate web of many complexities. Every person considers his own profession as the most important one. People may even consider other professions as lowly, unimportant and nurture careless, passive attitude towards other professions. The society is filled with a many people of varied nature. Only a very few, handful of seekers nurture the goal of Aparokṣānubhūti. Since, such seekers are very rare, it is wrong to conclude that their lives or life-styles may affect the society at large. This thought-process is meant for genuine seekers. It is not meant to cover up negative traits such as laziness, lethargy, ineptitude, failure, moodiness, sarcasism, emptiness, isolation or loneliness; and justify their lofty, contemptuous actions. We should not forget that St. Rāmadāsa, Tukārāma, Kabira, Tulasidāsa etc. have done enormous work for the society after Self-realization. It is necessary to also remember that they first attained the highest goal of liberation (Mokṣa) themselves, and then toiled for the society.

## Spiritual practices

**यमो हि नियमस्त्यागो मौनं देशश्च कालतः ।**

**आसनं मूलबन्धश्च देहसाम्यं च दृक्स्थितिः ॥ १०२ ॥**

*Yamo hi niyamastyāgo mounaṁ deśaśca kālataḥ /*

*Āsanaṁ mūlabandhaśca dehasamyaṅ ca dṛksthitiḥ // 102 //*

**प्राणसंयमनं चैव प्रत्याहारश्च धारणा ।**

**आत्मध्यानं समाधिश्च प्रोक्तान्यङ्गानि वै क्रमात् ॥ १०३ ॥**

*Prāṇasaṅyamanaṅ caiva Pratyāharśca Dhāraṇā /*

*Ātmādhyānaṁ samādhiśca proktānyaṅgani vai kramāt // 103 //*

**Meaning:** [Nididhyāsana means deep contemplation or meditation on Ātman.] The sequential aspects for Nididhyāsana are as follows: Control of the senses (Yama, यम), control of the mind (Niyama, नियम), renunciation (Tyāga, त्याग), internal silence (Mauna, मौन), place, time, posture (Āsana, आसन), the root lock (Mūlabandha, मूलबंध), equipoise of the body, steadiness of vision, control of the Prāṇa, control of the mind, power of concentration (Dhāraṇā, धारणा), meditation on Ātman (Ātmanusandhāna, आत्मानुसंधान) and complete absorption in Brahman (Samādhi, समाधी).

The practices mentioned in this verse are from the system of Asṭāṅgayoga (eight steps for union of Jīva with Ātman), which is useful for meditation practice. In this text, the spiritual practices of Asṭāṅgayoga are presented in the light of Advaita Vedānta. Ādi Śaṅkarācārya uses the same terms in Asṭāṅgayoga but gives them a new Vedāntic meaning as follows -

1. Yama (यम) - control of the sense organs
2. Niyama (नियम) - control of the mind (Antaḥkaraṇa)
3. Renunciation (त्याग) - not thinking about the worldly life, detachment
4. Silence (मौन) - not speaking and even thinking about space or time
5. Place (देश) - solitude by knowing that Brahman alone pervades everywhere
6. Time (काल) - the substratum of time is Brahman, undivided Pure Bliss

7. Āsana (आसन) - steady meditation on Brahman
8. Mūlabandha (मूलबंध) - concentration on Brahman, which is the very root of this universe.
9. Dehasāmya (देहसाम्य) - complete absorption of Jiva in One monolithic Brahman.
10. Dṛksthiti (दृक् स्थिती) - seeing Brahman everywhere. Disappearance of the triad of perceiver, perceived and perception

The worldly life (Prapañca, प्रपंच) is Preya (प्रेय) as stated in Katha Upaniṣad. It consists of two factors: the body and the world. They are perceivable (Dṛśya, दृश्य) and made up of the five great elements (Pañcamahābhūta). Even then, the body and the world are considered separate from each other for spiritual practice. One conducts his life with the help of his body and other entities in the world. Most people remain engrossed in thinking about the worldly matter throughout their lives. Spiritual practices are meant to stop the outward thinking and focus completely inward in Ātman. Both the body (Pinḍa-पिंड) and the world (Brahmānḍa-ब्रह्मांड) are perishable in nature. For realization of imperishable Ātman, it is necessary to discard all worldly thoughts in the mind. Ātman is (Pure) Existence, Consciousness, Bliss (Sat-Cit-Ānanda), which is real and eternal. Everything else is transient and insentient. All miseries in life are invariably related to transience and perishing. E.g. body, worldly objects, Jīva and circumstances are transient, and they are invariably associated with the pain of parting or dissociating from them. What if we can stop mental or emotional association with them in the first place (to avoid the pain of dissociation later)? Following spiritual practices help in this purpose -

- Prāṇayama (प्राणायाम) - controlling all manifestations of the mind
- Pratyāhāra (प्रत्याहार) - calmness of the mind due to seeing Ātman in all objects
- Dharaṇa (धारणा) - steady concentration in Ātman for a short period
- Dhyāna (ध्यान) - union of Jīva and Brahman for a short period of time
- Samādhi (समाधी) - complete, steady absorption in Ātman

## Yama

**सर्वं ब्रह्मेति विज्ञानादिन्द्रियग्रामसंयमः ।**

**यमोऽयमिति सम्प्रोक्तोऽभ्यसनीयो मुहुर्मुहुः ॥ १०४ ॥**

*Sarvaṁ Brahmeti vijñānādindriyagrāmasaṅyamaḥ /*

*Yamo'yamiti samprokto abhyāsānīyo muhurmuhuḥ // 104 //*

**Meaning:** Yama - With consistent thinking that 'everything is Brahman', one should control the five sense organs. Brahman is only One, monolithic, all-pervasive principle. There can be no division such as enjoyer and enjoyed, or knower and known, or perceiver and perceived in Brahman. This is called as real Yama. One should consistently think in this manner.

In traditional Asṭāṅgayoga, Yama indicates the rules regarding interactions with the world, such as restraining harmful physical urges, unwholesome mental thoughts and impulses. Yama includes non-killing, truthfulness, non-stealing, celibacy and not collecting unnecessary objects.

Here, Ādi Śaṅkarā describes Yama from a Vedāntic perspective, which is like the practice of Shabdānuviddha Samādhi (शब्दानुविद्ध समाधी, meditation with the help of words) as explained in the treatise of Dṛk Dṛśya Viveka.

## Niyama

सजातीयप्रवाहश्च विजातीयतिरस्कृतिः ।
नियमो हि परानन्दो नियमात्क्रियते बुधैः ॥ १०५ ॥

*Sajātīyapravāhaśca vijātīyatiraskṛtiḥ /*
*Niyamo hi parānando niyamātkriyate budhaiḥ // 105 //*

**Meaning:** Niyama - Consistent thinking as mentioned above is called as Niyama. It does not have a scope for any other thought. This is achievable only if all activities of the body and mind are stopped. This is a stage of Pure Bliss and all conscientious seekers practice it in the same manner.

In traditional Asṭāṅgayoga, Niyama indicates personal rules and cultivating good habits. Niyama includes being content with bare necessities of life, cleanliness, austerity, regular study of scriptures and the practice of surrendering to the God.

Here, Ādi Śaṅkarā describes Niyama as a continuous flow of thinking that 'I am Brahman and everything in the world is illusive in nature'. A sincere seeker who nurtures faith in Vedānta can discriminate between real-unreal, eternal-transient etc. He is wise in a true sense.

## Renunciation

त्यागः प्रपञ्चरूपस्य चिदात्मत्वावलोकनात् ।
त्यागो हि महतां पूज्यः सद्यो मोक्षमयो यतः ॥ १०६ ॥

*Tyāgaḥ prapañcarūpasya cidātmtvāvalokanāt /*
*Tyāgo hi mahatām pūjyaḥ sadyo Mokṣamayo yataḥ // 106 //*

**Meaning:** Thoughts about the worldly life involving names and forms automatically stop for the one, who has realized his real Self as Sat-Cit-Ānanda Brahman. Wise people call this type of renunciation as real renunciation. This is the very gist of Sadyomukti (सद्योमुक्ती).

Renunciation traditionally indicates giving up material belongings and officially adapting an ascetic way of life.

Here, Ādi Śaṅkarā describes renunciation from a Vedāntic perspective. He says that one is bound to experience the worldly life so long as the body is alive. When the five senses and the mind are active and awake, they are bound to experience the objects. Most people keep thinking about objects and whether they are good or bad. Renunciation as per Vedānta, is a state of the mind, where one firmly decides that all objects are transient and sublates (Badha, बाध) them. The firm thought of transience leads to gradual detachment from thinking about goodness or badness of objects. The practiotiner consequently becomes free from the duality of joy and grief. This type of renunciation is a result of the steady realization that 'I am Ātman (Pure Bliss)'. When illusions that 'I am body' and 'the world is real' disappear, the person becomes liberated in the very same moment.

## Silence

**यतो वाचो निवर्तन्ते अप्राप्य मनसा सह ।**
**यन्मौनं योगिभिर्गम्यं तद्भजेत्सर्वदा बुधः ॥ १०७ ॥**

*Yato vāco nivartante aprāpya manasā saha /*
*Yanmounaṁ yogibhirgamyam tadbhajetsarvadā budhaḥ // 107 //*

**Meaning:** Mind and speech (Vāṇī, वाणी) cannot realize Ātman, hence they retire completely. This silence (where mind and words are not present) is attainable by Yogis. Conscientious seekers should strive consistently to experience it.

Silence traditionally indicates complete cessation of the speech.

Here, Ādi Śaṅkarā describes the concept of silence based on a verse in Kena Upaniṣad -

**यन्मनसा न मनुते येनाहुर्मनो मतम् ।**
**तदेव ब्रह्म त्वं विद्धि नेदं यदिदमुपासते ॥**

*Yanmanusā na manute yenāhurmano matam /*
*Tadeva Brahma tvaṁ viddhi nedaṁ yadidamupāsate // (1.6)*

- That, which cannot be thought of by the mind, but by the order of which the mind thinks, is the one, all-pervasive Brahman.'

Ātman is called as the mind of the mind. In spiritual pursuit, the mind cannot comprehend Ātman. However, all desires in the mind arise on the substratum of Ātman. St. Jñāneśwara says that the mind floats on the branch of Rajoguṇa (Jñā. 13.104), which means the mind is made up of Rajoguṇa and impelled to function by Rajoguṇa. It is mistakenly considered that the mind is sentient since it has Cidābhāsa (Reflected Consciousness) in it. When the mind retires or disappears, one can experience complete silence. Seeker should verily experience this silence by conducting spiritual practice consistently as per the guidance of Sadguru and scriptures.

## The ultimate silence

वाचो यस्मान्निवर्तन्ते तद्वक्तुं केन शक्यते ।
प्रपञ्चो यदि वक्तव्यः सोऽपि शब्दविवर्जितः ॥ १०८ ॥

*Vāco yasmānnivartante tadvaktuṁ kena śakyate /*
*Prapañco yadi vaktavyaḥ so'pi śabdavivarjitaḥ // 108 //*

इति वा तद्भवेन्मौनं सतां सहजसंज्ञितम् ।
गिरा मौनं तु बालानां प्रयुक्तं ब्रह्मवादिभिः ॥ १०९ ॥

*Iti vā tadbhavenmounaṁ satāṁ sahajasañjnitam /*
*Girā mounaṁ tu bālānāṁ prayuktaṁ Brahmavādibhiḥ // 109 //*

**Meaning:** When speech is retired, how can one possibly describe Brahman? It is not possible to describe even the nature of the worldly life without the help of words. Ṛṣis say that even this indescribability of Brahman and the world is a kind of silence that is available naturally. Enlightened sages say that people who consider only 'absence of speech' as silence are childish (ignorant, immature) by nature.

The fundamental reason of silence is described here in this verse. St. Jñāneśwara says -

**या उपाधिमाजीं गुप्त । चैतन्य असे सर्वगत । तें तत्त्वज्ञ संत । स्वीकारिती ॥**

*Yā upādhimāji gupta / Caitanya ase sarvagata /*

*Te tatvajña santa / Swikāriti // (Jñā. 2-126)*

- Pure Consciousness (Caitanya, चैतन्य) is subtle and concealed. It pervades the body completely. However, only enlightened sages know it for real.

It is impossible to speak about Brahman that subtly pervades the body. Vāṇī (वाणी, speech organ) that strives to describe Brahman, retires along with the mind in the process of Self-realization. Both the mind (Antaḥkaraṇa) and Vāṇī are insentient. While meditating on Ātman, Cidābhāsa in the mind unites with its origin, Brahman (Reflected Consciousness merges into Pure Consciousness). The insentient mind and Vāṇī disappear at this point.

The process of acquiring worldly knowledge [Vṛittijñāna, वृत्तिज्ञान] is very different from realizing the Pure Knowledge of Ātman [Atmajñāna, आत्मज्ञान]. The process of worldly knowledge involves two steps –

***Vṛittivyāptī*** (वृत्तिव्याप्ती): Vṛitti is a ripple in the original calm state of the mind. Vṛitti arises in the mind when Jiva sees, hears, smells, touches or tastes an object. In everyday life, Vṛitti goes out through sense organs, pervades the object and acquires the same form as the object. This process is called as **Vṛittivyāptī.** The knowable object is initially covered by ignorance. Vṛitti removes the cover of ignorance from the knowable object. However, the object is not yet completely known by the knower at this stage.

***Phalavyāptī*** (फलव्याप्ती): Phala means Cidābhāsa i.e. Reflected Consciousness in the mind of the knower. Pure Consciousness (Ātman) is of the nature of the light. It pervades both the knower and the knowable. When Vṛitti removes the cover of ignorance from the object, the light of Cidābhāsa illumines the object. In other words, consciousness in the mind of the knower becomes one with the consciousness in the object. This enables the knower to know the object. The process of illumining (knowing) the object with the help of Reflected Consciousness is called as **Phalavyāptī**.

For knowledge in everyday life, both Vṛittivyāptī and Phalavyāptī are necessary. Vṛitti removes cover of ignorance on the object (Vṛittivyāptī) and Cidābhāsa illumines the object (Phalavyāptī).

However, for realization of Ātman, only Vṛittivyāptī is necessary. Phalavyāptī is not necessary. Ātman itself is the light of Pure Consciousness. In meditation, Vṛitti strives to seek Ātman, which is Vṛittivyāptī. When Vṛitti acquires the form of Ātman in meditation, the mind ceases to exist. Cidābhāsa (Reflected Consciousness) merges in its origin - Brahman (Pure Consciousness). Separate Phalavyāptī i.e. illumination by Cidābhāsa is not needed in this process, since Ātman, the knowable object, is Self-effulgent. Mind and all organs disappear completely in Self-realization; hence the process is beyond explanation or expression. This is the concept of real silence explained in the verse.

Ātman does not have Prāṇa, sense organs or the mind (Aprāṇa-अप्राण, Ajivha-अजिह्व, Amana-अमन) as described in Muṇḍaka Upaniṣad (1.1.6). Hence, the concept of speaking about Ātman is moot. This is the definition of real silence.

Māṇḍūkya Kārikā has taken a standpoint that -

**प्रपंचो यदि विद्येत निवर्तेत न संशयः ।**

*Prapañco yadi vidyeta nivarteta na sañśayaḥ / (1.17)*

- If the world had existed for real, it would have been possible to eradicate it. (However, since it cannot be discarded or eradicated, it does not have real existence.)

This verse (108) is apparently saying the same thing as mentioned in this Māṇḍūkya Kārikā. The insentient world full of names and forms cannot be described without words. Vāṇī (वाणी, speech organ) cannot say anything unless it is associated with the mind, Cidābhāsa and Prāṇas. Jīva must impel the Vāṇī to speak. The transactional life takes place with help of the mind and speech. However, when Jīva becomes One with Brahman, who will impel or dictate the Vāṇī to speak?

Alternate meaning in this verse indicates that the nature of the world is very vast and expansive. Hence Vāṇī is incapable of speaking about it in a comprehensive manner, which is evident.

There are primarily two meanings of these verses. The first meaning says that the Vāṇī retires due to union of Jīva with Brahman. The second meaning says that the mind and Vāṇī are incapable of comprehending and describing the vast, expansive nature of the world.

Ādi Śaṅkarācārya says in this verse that both these meanings indicate the real silence. The prevalent meaning of silence, which indicates 'deliberate cessation of speech or absence of words' is a childish interpretation of the concept of silence. Some people who maintain this so-called silence, try to communicate by writing on paper. Novice seekers practice silence by not speaking, however, it is the preliminary stage of silence and should not be ridiculed. This verse states that silence of the mind is more important than the absence of speech. The two meanings of silence described in this verse indicate the final stage of enlightenment.

## Solitude (Ekānta)

आदावन्ते च मध्ये च जनो यस्मिन्न विद्यते ।
येनेदं सततं व्याप्तं स देशो विजनः स्मृतः ॥ ११० ॥

*Adāvante ca madhye ca jano yasminna vidyate /*
*Yenedaṁ satataṁ vyāptaṁ sa deso vijanaḥ smṛtaḥ // 110 //*

**Meaning:** A place, where the world does not exist in the beginning, middle or end, and which is always pervaded (by One non-dual Brahman), may be called as the solitude.

Solitude traditionally means a lonely or uninhabited place. It also indicates the state or situation of being alone.

Ādi Śaṅkarā describes the concept of solitude in Rājayoga (the path of Knowledge) here. Human beings are always aware of the world and life within the boundaries of the space and time. Every object or person undergoes birth, life and death. Even the universe has beginning, existence for some time and end. This itself is limitation by time (Kāla-Pariccheda, कालपरिच्छेद) and limitation by space (Desha-Pariccheda, देशपरिच्छेद). Brahman, as if, is itself the vast, all-pervasive solitude, where there is no trace of the material world. There is no 'second' in the realm of Brahman. Ādi Śaṅkarā says in this verse that knowing the One, all-pervasive, non-dual Brahman is the pinnacle of enjoying solitude.

## Time (Kāla)

**कलनात् सर्वभूतानां ब्रह्मादीनां निमेषतः ।**
**कालशब्देन निर्दिष्टो ह्यखण्डानन्दकोऽद्वयः ॥ १११ ॥**

*Kalanāt sarvabhūtanāṁ Brahmādīnāṁ nimeṣataḥ /*
*Kālaśabdena nirdiṣṭo hyakhanḍānandako'dvayaḥ // 111 //*

**Meaning:** In a flash, Brahman creates a seamless mixture (like mud) of Brahmadeva and other beings, and the entire universe from that (mixture). The word 'time' indicates non-dual Brahman, which is undivided Pure Bliss.

Traditionally, the word 'time' is used to indicate indefinite or continuous duration or period. It is often referred to as a fourth dimension, along with the three spatial dimensions.

Ādi Śaṅkarā describes the concept of time based in Brahman here. Brahmasūtra describes Brahman as -

अविभागेन दृष्टत्वात् ।

*Avibhāgena Driṣṭatvat / (4.4.4)*

- A liberated Jīva is not separate from Brahman.

St. Jñāneśwara says –

भरला घनदाट हरी दिसे ।

*Bharalā ghanadāṭa hari dise /*

- I see only God (Brahman) everywhere without any space in between.

Brahman is without separations, divisions or duality of any kind. The indivisible, monolithic nature of Brahman is explained in more detail here. The nature of Brahman is deliberately denoted by the word Pure Bliss (Ānanda, happiness regardless of anything or anyone) and seekers are propelled to revel in continuous, perpetual, Pure Bliss of Brahman. The verse says that all spiritual practices lead the seeker in the same direction of reveling in Pure Bliss. Otherwise, the concept of time (Kāla, काल) is only imaginary and some scholars state that the universe is created from it.

## Posture (Āsana)

सुखेनैव भवेद्यस्मिन्नजस्रं ब्रह्मचिन्तनम् ।
आसनं तद्विजानीयान्नेतरत्सुखनाशनम् ॥ ११२ ॥

*Sukhenaiva bhavedyasminnajasraṁ Brahmacintanam /*
*Asanaṁ tadvijanīyānnetaratsukhanāśanam // 112 //*

**Meaning:** The posture in which one can steadily remain and meditate on Brahman is the real Āsana (posture). (On the other hand) The posture in which one experiences (physical) pain or discomfort is not the real Āsana.

In traditional Asṭāṅgayoga, Āsana indicates a posture that enables one to sit easily in one position for prolonged meditation. Many Yoga teachers and Sampradāyās teach many types of postures and Āsanas. The main objective for them, is that the body should remain healthy and disease-free. Those who practice Asṭāṅgayoga Āsanas even get the benefit of that practice.

However, consistent, steady contemplation (Nididhyāsana) on Brahman is a gradual, delicate process. It is expected to last for a long duration, so physical strain should not create obstacle in its practice. Ādi Śaṅkarā says in this verse that the contemplation on Brahman is the main objective, while ability to sit steady is a peripheral issue. Hence, a seeker should sit in a posture, in which he is most comfortable. The posture should not lead to numbness of feet, or strain in muscles or other body parts. With growing age, there may be difficulty in sitting in one posture. So, one should take help of chair, back-rest etc. However, one should not lie down or sit in a loose, casual posture for meditating on Brahman.

## Steady Brahmāsana is the real Āsana

सिद्धं यत्सर्वभूतादि विश्वाधिष्ठानमव्ययम् ।
यस्मिन्सिद्धाः समाविष्टास्तद्वै सिद्धासनं विदुः ॥ ११३ ॥

*Siddhaṁ yatsarvabhūtādi visvādhiṣṭhanamavyayam |*
*Yasminsiddhāḥ samaviṣṭastadvai siddhāsanaṁ viduḥ || 113 ||*

**Meaning:** Brahman is the very root (origin) of all sentient and insentient entities in the world. All enlightened people are completely unified in Brahman, which is the formless substratum of the world. This verily is known as the Siddhāsana.

In AṣṭaṅgaYoga, Siddhāsana is the name of one physical posture.

However, as per the system of Rājayoga described by Ādi Śaṅkarā in this verse, Siddhāsana indicates Brahman, which is the real nature of everything in the universe. Brahman is ever-existent (NityaSiddha, नित्यसिद्ध). It does not depend on any scientific proof or logical validation. Brahman is objective, not subjective. From Vedāntic perspective, the union of Jiva with ever-existent Brahman is the real Siddhāsana. Here the word 'Āsana' is used just for formality. It is not even remotely related to any posture or condition of the body or the mind. Bhagvad-Gītā calls it as Dhāma (place of residence) -

यद् गत्वा न निवर्तन्ते तद्धाम परमं मम ।

*Yad gattvā na nivartante taddhāma paramaṁ mama | (15.6)*

\- (Brahman is) That place after reaching where, one does not ever have to return.

## Root Lock (Mūlabandha)

यन्मूलं सर्वभूतानां यन्मूलं चित्तबन्धनम् ।
मूलबन्धः सदा सेव्यो योग्योऽसौ राजयोगिनाम् ॥ ११४ ॥

*Yanmūlaṁ sarvabhūtānaṁ yanmūlaṁ cittabandhanam /*
*Mūlabandhaḥ sadā sevyo yogyo 'sou Rājayoginām // 114 //*

**Meaning:** Brahman (Sat, Pure Existence) is the real root of the existence of the universe. It is the very substratum of calmness of the mind. The mind is binded on Brahman itself. The seekers of Rājayoga should take refuge only in Brahman.

The word Mūla means root. Bandha means binding or a lock. In traditional AṣṭaṅgaYoga, Mūlabandha indicates a Yoga practice that involves constraining, contracting and locking the area around perineal body. It is one of the three bindings (Bandhas) that are used to control the five Prāṇas and direct that energy in the desired direction.

However, in Rājayoga as described by Ādi Śaṅkarā, Mūlabandha means binding the mind with Brahman, which is the root of this universe. Alternatively, it means absorption of the mind (Citta, चित्त) in Pure Consciousness (Shuddha Caitanya, शुद्ध चैतन्य).

Vedanta states that the world is falsely superimposed (Adhyasta) on Brahman -

- Existence (Astitva-अस्तित्व) of the world - Sat (Pure Existence)

- Perception (Bhatitva-भातित्व) of the world - Cit (Pure Knowledge)
- Likeability (Priyatva-प्रियत्व) of the worldly objects - Ananda (Pure Bliss)

Adhyasta is naturally bound by Adhiṣṭhāna. Hence, the superimposed world is naturally bound by substratum Brahman. On an individual level, superimposed Jiva is bound by the substratum Ātman. Ādi Śaṅkarā says here that the mind (Citta, चित्त) is bound for real, only when it disappears in Pure Consciousness. All seekers of Rājayoga should try to attain Mūlabandha (मूलबंध) of this kind.

## Equipoise of the Body (Dehasamya)

अङ्गानां समतां विद्यात्समे ब्रह्मणि लीयते ।

नो चेन्नैव समानत्वमृजुत्वं शुष्कवृक्षवत् ॥ ११५ ॥

*Aṅganām samatām vidyātsame Brahmaṇi līyate /*

*No cennaiva samānatvamṛjutvam śuṣkavṛkṣavat // 115 //*

**Meaning:** When Jīva is completely absorbed in the One, monolithic Brahman, it is called as the equipoise of organs (body). Mere sitting straight just like a dried-up tree, should not be called as equipoise.

## Vision (Driṣṭi)

दृष्टिं ज्ञानमयीं कृत्वा पश्येद्ब्रह्ममयं जगत् ।

सा दृष्टिः परमोदारा न नासाग्रावलोकिनी ॥ ११६ ॥

*Dṛṣṭim jñānamayim kṛtva pasyedbrahmamayam jagat /*

*Sa dṛṣṭiḥ parmodārā na nāsāgrāvalokinī // 116 //*

द्रष्टृदर्शनदृश्यानां विरामो यत्र वा भवेत् ।

दृष्टिस्तत्रैव कर्तव्या न नासाग्रावलोकिनी ॥ ११७ ॥

*Draṣṭṛdarśanadṛśyanām virāmo yatra vā bhavet /*
*Dṛṣṭistatraiva kartavyā na nāsāgrāvalokini // 117 //*

**Meaning:** Seeing Brahman in the entire world is the most noble vision. It does not involve focusing on the tip of the nose. It involves merging of the triad of perceiver, perceived and perception (Draṣṭā, Driṣṭi, Dṛśya) into One Brahman. This vision should be consciously acquired. It is not necessary to focus on the tip of the nose.

In Aṣṭaṅgayoga, the word Dṛṣṭi means steady and firm vision that is achieved by focusing the eyes on the tip of the nose or the middle of the eyebrows etc. It helps in concentration of the mind.

In this verse, Ādi Śaṅkarācārya states that one should strive to make the triad of perceiver, perceived and perception (Draṣṭā, Dṛśya, Dṛṣṭi) disappear and merge in Brahman. Dṛṣṭi here, indicates that one should watch the entire world as if it is only Brahman everywhere (and nothing else).

There is a verse in Bṛihadāraṇyaka Upaniṣad -

न हि द्रष्टुर्दृष्टेः विपरिलोपो विद्यते ।

*Na hi draṣṭurdṛuṣṭeḥ viparilopo vidyāte / (4.3.23)*

- The vision of the perceiver never ceases, since the perceiver is imperishable. Nothing is separate from the perceiver that can be perceived.

Such vision of Pure Knowledge (Brahman) is difficult to obtain due to the veil of Māyā. Hence, one should discard or sublate the manifestations of Māyā and look at the world with complete Knowledge of Brahman.

## Regulating the breath (Prāṇayama)

चित्तादिसर्वभावेषु ब्रह्मत्वेनैव भावनात् ।
निरोधः सर्ववृत्तीनां प्राणायामः स उच्यते ॥ ११८ ॥

*Cittadisarvabhāveṣu Brahmatvenaiva bhāvanāt /*
*Nirodhaḥ sarvavṛttīnām Prāṇāyāmaḥ sa ucyate // 118 //*

**Meaning:** To know firmly that the mind and its other manifestations are all verily Brahman, and thereby control them is called as Prāṇayama.

In Aṣṭaṅgayoga, Prāṇayama is the technique of rhythmic breathing to gain control of Prāṇas (life forces).

In this verse, Ādi Śaṅkarā explains Prāṇayama from the perspective of Rājayoga. Mind, intellect, memory and ego (मन, बुद्धि, चित्त, अहंकार) are the four manifestations of Antaḥkaraṇa (अंतःकरण). They function with the help of Cidābhāsa and Prāṇas. Even the subtlest movement of the body or the mind does not take place without Prāṇa. Kena Upaniṣad says that Ātman is the Prāṇa of Prāṇa (1.2). Thus, Prāṇas function only on the substratum of Ātman. Cidābhāsa is just the reflection of Pure Consciousness in the mind. When the four manifestations of Antaḥkaraṇa (Vṛtti) retire and cease to exist, Cidābhāsa becomes one with its real Self i.e. Ātman. In other words, Reflected Consciousness becomes one with Pure Consciousness since the medium of reflection (mind) is retired. When the mind disappears in Brahman, Prāṇa that supports the mind disappearas well. This itself is the real Prāṇayama. Prāṇas, which support the functioning of the body, continue their work in a routine manner in this process.

## Types of Prāṇayama

निषेधनं प्रपञ्चस्य रेचकाख्यः समीरणः ।
ब्रह्मैवास्मीति या वृत्तिः पूरको वायुरीरितः ॥ ११९॥

*Niṣedhanaṁ prapañcasya recakākhyaḥ samīraṇaḥ /*
*Brahmaivāsmīti yā vṛtti pūrako vayurīritaḥ //119 //*

ततस्तद्वृत्तिनैश्चल्यं कुंभकः प्राणसंयमः ।
अयं चापि प्रबुद्धानामज्ञानां घ्राणपीडनम् ॥ १२०॥

*Tatastadvṛttinaiścalyaṁ kumbhakaḥ Prāṇa saṁyamaḥ /*
*Ayaṁ cāpi prabuddhānāmajñānam ghrāṇapīdanam //120 //*

**Meaning:** Withdrawal of the world (in thoughts) is Rechak Prāṇayama. The thought that 'I am Brahman' is Puraka Prāṇayama. The consequent steadiness of the mind is Kumbhaka Prāṇayama. This is nature of real Prāṇayama done by enlightened sages. Ignorant people only torture the nose by pressing the nostrils.

In Aṣṭaṅgayoga, Rechaka means exhalation, Puraka means inhalation and Kumbhaka means holding the breath. These are rhythmic breathing techniques of Prāṇayama that are used to control life forces.

According the Vedānta, Rechaka means exhaling (refuting) the thought that 'the world is real', Puraka means inhaling (embracing) the thought that 'Brahman alone is real' and Kumbhaka means holding the inhaled thought steadily and consistently. The word 'Prāṇa' is used in Patanjali Yogasūtras to indicate life forces. However, it is used to explain the attainment of Self-realization using the path of Knowledge in this treatise. This verse primarily talks about Brahman, which is the Prāṇa of Prāṇa. Prāṇas derive their characteristic of 'life forces' only from Brahman. Ādi Śaṅkarācārya does not intend to mock those practitioners, who press the nostrils to conduct Prāṇayama. His main intention is to show the glory and prosperity of those who have realized Brahman as the real Self. It is important to remember that Ādi Śaṅkara was a great Yogi himself.

## Control of the mind (Pratyāhāra)

विषयेष्वात्मतां दृष्ट्वा मनसश्चितिमज्जनम् ।

प्रत्याहारः स विज्ञेयोऽभ्यसनीयो मुमुक्षुभिः ॥ १२१ ॥

*Vishayesvātmatāṁ dṛṣṭva manasaścitimajjanam /*

*Pratyāharaḥ sa vijñeyo'bhyasanīyo mumukṣubhiḥ //121//*

**Meaning:** The mind becomes calm with the firm realization that Ātman pervades all worldly objects that can be known with senses. This (calmness of the mind) is called as Pratyāhāra. All seekers of Mokṣa should practice it consistently.

In Aṣṭaṅgayoga, Pratyāhara means withdrawing the senses from their objects of enjoyment.

In Rajayaoga, Ādi Śaṅkarācārya says that Pratyāhara is seeing Ātman in all objects. The world is known with the help of nine Pramāṇas such as perception, inference, analogy etc. (pratyakṣa, anumāna, upamāna etc.). Due to ignorance, the world is seen as real, and (ignorant) mind always thinks about people, objects and other worldly issues. However, Vedānta says -

**सर्वं खल्विदं ब्रह्म ।**

*Sarvaṁ khalvidaṁ Brahman / (Chan. Up. 3.14.1)*

- Everything in the world is verily Brahman.

Thus, all objects that can be denoted, represented or indicated, are Brahman in essence. St. Jñāneśwara says that both Idanta (objects denoted by he, she, it, this, that) and Ahanta (I, me, mine) are verily Brahman. Idam (he, she, it, this, that) is with respect to the world, while Aham (I, me, mine) is with respect to an individual. They are both manifestations of ignorance, but they are only Brahman, and nothing else. With this firm belief, mind becomes calm and stable. This is the real Pratyāhāra. All seekers of liberation should practice attaining it.

## Focus (Dharaṇa)

**यत्र यत्र मनो याति ब्रह्मणस्तत्र दर्शनात् ।**
**मनसो धारणा चैव धारणा सा परा मता ॥ १२२ ॥**

*Yatra yatra mano yāti Brahmaṇastatra darśanāt /*
*Manaso dhāraṇā caiva dhāraṇā sā parā matā // 122 //*

**Meaning:** Firmly adhering to the decision that everything perceived, known or persuaded by the mind is verily Brahman, is known as the supreme Dharaṇa.

In Aṣṭaṅgayoga, Dharaṇa is fixing the mind on the object of meditation, such as a picture or a flame etc.

Here, Adi Śaṅkara says that Dharaṇa means fixing the mind on Brahman. It is the job of the intellect (Buddhi, बुद्धि) to make a decision and stick to it. St. Jñāneśwara says in his treatise, 'when the decision of the intellect is synchronized with the one-pointed mind absorbed in Brahman, the seeker sees Brahman everywhere'. This is the nature of Dharaṇa as propounded by the path of Knowledge in Vedānta. It is also known as Rājayoga (Jñānayoga).

## Meditation (Dhyāna)

ब्रह्मैवास्मीति सद्वृत्त्या निरालम्बतया स्थितिः ।
ध्यानशब्देन विख्याता परमानन्ददायिनी ॥ १२३ ॥

*Brahmaivāsmiti sadvṛttya nirālambatayā sthitiḥ /*
*Dhyānaśabdena vikhyātā paramānandadāyinī // 123 //*

**Meaning:** Dhyāna is remaining steady in the impenetrable thought that 'I am Brahman' without the support or contact of anything else. This (state) gives the experience of Supreme Bliss to Jīva (who practices Dhyāna).

In Aṣṭaṅgayoga, Dhyāna means uninterrupted meditation or intense mental concentration.

So far, all definitions in this treatise describe the sequential, progressive ladder of spiritual pratices for the direct, steady realization that 'I am Brahman'. The process of practicing Dhyāna in this verse is described by Ādi Śaṅkarācārya as per the path of Vedāntic knowledge. It states that, Dhyāna is the stage, where one uninterruptedly remains absorbed in the steady realization of Mahāvākya 'I am Brahman', which is Pure Bliss. In this stage, Jīva who normally dwells in the duality of (worldly) joy and grief, becomes One with Brahman and enjoys the Supreme, Pure Bliss of Brahman. Mind and ego (Ahaṅkāra) disappear in Brahman in this stage. The entire phenomenal world (Dṛśya, दृश्य) is based in ego (Ahaṅkāra, अहंकार). Once, the ego disappears, the world becomes inconsequential as well. The practitioner has no support or contact of any worldly thought or entity in this stage. Jīva, which is born, raised and connected with the world, ultimately leaves the support of the worldly thoughts and entities, and becomes One with Ātman, his real Self. He is Pure Bliss himself at this stage. In other words, Jīva becomes Ānandarūpa (आनंदरूप, Bliss is his very nature), Sukharūpa (सुखरूप, personification of happiness), Ātmakrīḍa (आत्मक्रीड, in everyday transactional life, he feels as if he is playing with Brahman itself) and Ātmarati (आत्मरती, soaked in Brahman, revels in the Pure Bliss of Brahman).

## Samādhi

निर्विकारतया वृत्त्या ब्रह्माकारतया पुनः ।
वृत्तिविस्मरणं सम्यक्समाधिर्ज्ञानसंज्ञकः ॥ १२४ ॥

*Nirvikāratayā vṛttya Brahmākāratayā punaḥ /*
*Vṛttivismaraṇam samyaksamādhirjñānasañjñakaḥ // 124 //*

**Meaning:** Samādhi is the stage of absolute, unchanging union with Brahman, where Antaḥkaraṇa (mind) is completely absorbed in Brahman. It is the Pure, Absolute Knowledge itself.

In Aṣṭaṅgayoga, Samadhi is the total absorption of the mind in the object of meditation.

In Rājayoga, Samadhi is the total absorption of the mind in Brahman. Samādhi is said to be attained when Dhyāna matures completely. It is not possible to express the fact that 'I am in Samādhi'. The moment such a thought arises, Samādhi is interrupted and Jīva again becomes aware of himself as a limited being. Presence of any thought indicates Vṛitti (modification in the mind). Samādhi is the stage when the mind (Antaḥkaraṇa, अंतःकरण) completely disappears (ceases to function), and there is no trace of Vṛttijñāna (वृत्तिज्ञान, qualified knowledge gained with the triad of knower, knowable, knowledge). Jīva is completely absorbed in Brahman. Ignorance does not even remotely exist in Samādhi. This stage is like the state of deep-sleep in some way, where Jīva cannot explain that 'I am in deep-sleep', and Jīva has no knowledge of his own body-mind or other worldly issues. However, according to Vedānta, the deep-sleep consists of complete ignorance (Ghan-Ajñāna, घन-अज्ञान). St. Tukārāma says in one of his compositions –

गेले भावाभाव झाला स्वयमेव पांडुरंग ।

*Gele bhāvabhāva Jhālā swayameva Pāṇḍuraṅga /*

- Now (after Self-realization), all ideas of existence or non-existence (w.r.t. body) are eradicated. I am one with Pāṇḍuraṅga (Brahman).

Persistent practice in this manner leads to Iccha Samādhi (इच्छा समाधी), where the person can attain Samādhi at his will in any place or time.

## Samādhi at will

**एवञ्चाकृत्रिमानन्दं तावत्साधु समभ्यसेत् ।**
**वश्यो यावत्क्षणात्पुंसः प्रयुक्तः सन् भवेत्स्वयम् ॥ १२५ ॥**

*Evañcakṛtrimānandaṁ tāvatsādhu samabhyaset /*
*Vaśyo yāvatkṣānatpuṅsaḥ prayuktaḥ san bhavetswayam // 125 //*

**Meaning:** The seeker of Mokṣa (Mumukṣu, मुमुक्षु) should try to attain Samādhi that gives him ever-available Pure Bliss, with the help of the subtle mind. Later, (with consistent practice), the seeker can attain it anytime at will.

Dharaṇa, Dhyāna and Samādhi need to be practiced with the subtle mind (Sukṣma Antaḥkaraṇa Vṛtti, सूक्ष्म अंतःकरणवृत्ती). For that purpose, one must purposefully control desires of gross objects. This is the real benefit of practicing Yama, Niyama, Pratyāhāra as explained in earlier verses. With the help of these practices, the mind becomes progressively subtler. Only then it gets ready for its own disappearance. Once the mind is retired (in meditation), its substratum Ātman is realized, and the ever-shining light of the Pure Knowledge of Ātman is unveiled.

St. Rāmadāsa says - being alert about one's own real Self (Brahman), is the indication of real, Pure Knowledge.

Reveling in Pure Bliss propels the seeker towards more, deeper practice, and eventually he is able to attain Samādhi at ease and at will. This natural, instinctive realization of Samādhi is highly important in spiritual pursuit. The mature seeker (enlightened person) can practice it at will, at any time, in any place and in all circumstances. Once the goal of Mokṣa is achieved, every spiritual practice becomes inconsequential.

## A third person cannot recognize a Yogi

ततः साधननिर्मुक्तः सिद्धो भवति योगिराट् ।
तत्स्वरूपं न चैतस्य विषयो मनसो गिराम् ॥ १२६ ॥

*Tataḥ sādhananirmuktaḥ siddho bhāvati yogirāṭ /*
*Tatswarūpaṁ na caitasya viṣayo manaso girām // 126 //*

**Meaning:** It is not possible to comprehend by mind, or to verbally describe the nature of an enlightened, great Yogi, who is liberated from all spiritual practices.

A Self-realized person or a great Yogi does not depend on any extrinsic factor for his realized state. St. Rāmadāsa says in his treatise that only an enlightened person can know the makings of another enlightened person (Dāsabodha 1.4.31). All spiritual practices wear away for him, and he leads his life like other ordinary people. Most people cannot guess his real level or state. His life has no external aspect that reflects his enlightened state. Bhagvad-Gītā tells the state of such a person with the verse-

**अद्वेष्टा सर्वभूतानां मैत्रः करुण एव च ।**

*Adveṣṭa sarva bhutānām maitraḥ karuṇa eva ca / (12.13)*

- He (Self-realized sage) feels no resentment for anyone and only feels empathy for one and all. Every being is his friend (he has no enemies). These indications of his nature are understood only when one stays in his company for a long time.

Ātman is formless, mindless, attributeless and speechless. One who realizes Ātman may have ordinary physical external appearance. But internally, he is One with the formless Ātman. He may have many external qualities, but internally he is attributeless (Nirguṇa, निर्गुण). He cannot be described by routine ways of description. Ātman is Self-effulgent, so one who realizes Ātman, becomes Self-effulgent as well. Ordinary people cannot recognize him with the help of five senses, mind, or other routine means of gaining knowledge (Pramaṇas, प्रमाण).

After describing these gratifying traits of Self-realization, Ādi Śaṅkarācārya now describes many obstacles in the way of attaining the ultimate Samādhi.

## Obstacles in attainment of Samādhi

**समाधौ क्रियमाणे तु विघ्नान्यायान्ति वै बलात् ।**
**अनुसन्धानराहित्यमालस्यं भोगलालसम् ॥ १२७ ॥**

*Samādhou kriyamāṇe tu vighnānyāyānti vai balāt /*

*Anusandhānarāhityamālasyaṁ bhogalālasam || 127 ||*

लयस्तमश्च विक्षेपो रसास्वादश्च शून्यता ।

एवं यद्विघ्नबाहुल्यं त्याज्यं ब्रह्मविदा शनैः ॥ १२८ ॥

*Layastamśca vikṣepo rasāsvādaśca sūnyata |*

*Evam yadvighnabāhulyaṁ tyājyaṁ Brahmavidā sanaiḥ || 128 ||*

**Meaning:** Many obstacles invariably arise while the seeker strives to practice and attain Samādhi. For example, lack of constant connection with Ātman, lethargy, craving for sense-pleasures, sleep, wavering nature, dullness of the intellect, tasting of intermittent joy, experience of void etc. One should gradually overcome these obstacles in order to gain the Knowledge of Brahman.

1. **Lack of Anusandhāna** (अनुसंधान, constant connection with Ātman) - The word Anusandhāna consists of the prefix Anu (अनु), which means constant pursual. The word, Sandhāna (संधान) means holding on to something firmly. In the context of Samādhi, the word Anusandhāna means the subtle mind (Sukṣma Antaḥkaraṇa Vṛtti, सूक्ष्म अंतःकरण वृत्ती) pursues Ātman constantly and adheres to it firmly. This constant flow of the subtle mind towards Ātman may get broken due to many reasons. These reasons are caused by identification of Jīva with the body (Dehatādātmya, देहतादात्म्य), and believing that 'the world is real' (Jagat Satyatva, जगत्सत्यत्व). For example, physical pain, disease or familial problems become obstacle in Anusandhāna of Brahman. The seeker should first get rid of the physical pain by appropriate treatment and solve the

familial problems. If it is not possible to solve the problems, then he should learn to ignore them to overcome this obstacle in Samādhi.

2. **Lethargy** - This is one of the characteristic properties of Tamoguṇa. Only one who intensely pines for attainment of Samādhi, can get rid of lethargy with firm resolution.
3. **Craving for sense pleasures** - This is a natural human tendency and one may have it in less or more proportion. The joy that one finds in material objects may be instantaneous, however it is not perpetual. It is transient and comes to end sooner or later. On the contrary, the Pure Bliss of Samādhi is perpetual in nature. The seeker should consciously understand this fundamental concept explained in scriptures, give up the desires for temporary sense pleasures, and strive to attain the eternal, Pure Bliss of Samādhi.
4. **Sleepiness** - There are many instances of people feeling sleepy while listening to spiritual discourses, devotional songs, reading or traveling. Same thing may happen in the practice of Samādhi. This obstacle can be overcome by maintaining good health, getting adequate sleep in night, and practicing for Samādhi in early morning hours.
5. **Dullness of the intellect** - If all physical movements, thoughts, reading, comprehension etc. are dull and passive, then one should make resolute efforts to increase their efficiency.

6. **Wavering mind** - This is an invariable result of Rajoguṇa. It can be avoided by consciously keeping away from food, company, reading and other aspects that fuel the Rajoguṇa. This obstacle can also be overcome with regular worship (Upāsanā) of the God in some way.
7. **Tasting of occassional joy** - As a seeker progresses in the practice of Samādhi, he may occasionally experience joy (Rasāswāda) as a result of increasing concentration and quietning of the mind. However, this joy is very transient and small as compared to the ultimate, Pure Bliss of Self-realization. One needs to be alert and vigilant to overcome this obstacle in the practice of Samādhi.
8. **Void** - One may experience an intermittent stage of void, when seeker is disconnected from the world, but not yet unified with Brahman. This is the sign of dull intellect. This can be avoided by carefully following the guidance of Sadguru.

The seeker should thus strive to overcome these obstacles steadily by staying careful and vigilant about his own practice and progress. Samarth Rāmdāsa Swāmi says, 'one who is alert, consistent and vigilant, will immediately attain Mokṣa.'

## Practice for complete absorption in Brahman

भाववृत्त्या हि भावत्वं शून्यवृत्त्या हि शून्यता ।
ब्रह्मवृत्त्या हि पूर्णत्वं तथा पूर्णत्वमभ्यसेत् ॥ १२९ ॥

*Bhāvavṛttya hi bhāvatvam śūnyavṛttya hi śūnyata /*
*Brahmavṛtya hi pūrṇatvam tatha pūrṇatvamabhyaset // 129 //*

**Meaning:** When the mind thinks about objects, it identifies with the objects (extrovertness). When the mind thinks about void (Śūnya, शून्य) it identifies with the void. However, when the mind thinks about Brahman, it becomes One with Brahman. Hence, the seeker should only study Brahman to attain the ultimate completeness.

St. Rāmadāsa says that those who contemplate on the real Self, can transcend the worldly life and reach the ultimate stage of Self-realization (Dās. 18.1.24). Those who do not contemplate on the Self, sink in the ocean of worldly life. People who are not introvert and contemplative by nature, keep thinking about the material objects (Dṛśya, दृश्य) all their life. They do not understand the triad of perceiver, perceived, perception (Draṣṭā, Dṛśya, Darshan). People, who tend to sleep or think about the void (Śūnya) as described above, lead a meaningless and empty life. Those who consistently contemplate on Mahāvākya *Aham Brahmāsmi* and practice Soham meditation, become Brahman themselves. St. Jñāneśwara says in his treatise that, the one who is in constant connection with Brahman, becomes Brahman in person. Upaniṣad says that Brahman is complete (Purnamadah purnamidam, पूर्णमदः पूर्णमिदं). So, one who strives for being One with Brahman, becomes complete by realizing that 'I am Brahman'.

## Meaningless human life

ये हि वृत्तिं जहत्येनां ब्रह्माख्यां पावनीं पराम् ।
वृथैव ते तु जीवन्ति पशुभिश्च समा नराः ॥ १३० ॥

*Ye hi vṛttiṁ jahatyenām Brahmākhyāṁ pavanīṁ parāṁ /*
*Vruthaiva te tu jīvanti paśubhiśca samā narāḥ // 130 //*

**Meaning:** Thus, people who do not uphold or maintain this most purifying thought of Brahman, live a meaningless, vain life. Even though born as humans, they lead only animal life.

The life of various species such as birds, beasts, animals, aquatic animals, virus, bacteria, mosquitoes etc. is evidently seen by one and all. Their lives are very limited on both spiritual as well as worldly front. They are not even remotely concerned with evolved aspects such as poetry, art, sports, literature, beauty etc. A conscientious person may see delicate art in sea-shells or conches, intricate beauty in bird-nests, melody in their chirping, and discipline in the movement of ants. However, these asepcts are not even slightly related to spiritual pursuit. St. Rāmadāsa Swāmi summarizes the supreme goal of human life in the concluding verse of his treatise -

निर्गुण ब्रह्म ते निश्चळ । अंतरी बिंबले ॥

*Nirguṇa Brahma te niśhala / Antari bimbale // (20.10.26)*

- Now I have realized that my real Self is the attributeless, formless and immovable Brahman.

## The supreme goal

ये हि वृत्तिं विजानन्ति ज्ञात्वापि वर्धयन्ति ये ।

ते वै सत्पुरुषा धन्या वन्द्यास्ते भुवनत्रये ॥ १३१ ॥

*Ye hi vṛttiṁ vijānanti jñātvāpi vardhayanti ye /*

*Te vai satpuruṣā dhanyā vandyāste bhuvanatraye // 131 //*

**Meaning:** Enlightened people who first realize their real Self as Brahman, and then contemplate on it steadily, are indeed blessed. They are respected everywhere in the three plains (Bhuvanas - Swarga, Bhu, Patala).

The concept of a meaningful, high-quality life is different in the worldly and spiritual context. Successful, glorious life is largely dependent on Prārabdha (प्रारब्ध) in the worldly sense, while it is entirely dependent on conscious efforts in the spiritual pursuit. St. Tukārāma Mahārāja led a poverty-stricken worldly life, while King Janaka lead a very prosperous, glorious life as a king. However, from spiritual perspective, they were the same. They both realized their real Self as Brahman (Vitthala, विठ्ठल) and led a very content, meaningful life replete with joy and Pure Bliss.

## Mere theoretical knowledge is of no use

येषां वृत्तिः समावृद्धा परिपक्वा च सा पुनः ।

ते वै सद्ब्रह्मतां प्राप्ता नेतरे शब्दवादिनः ॥ १३२ ॥

*Yeṣām vṛttiḥ samāvṛddhā paripakvā ca sā punaḥ /*

*Te vai sad Brahmatām prāptā netare śabdavādinaḥ // 132 //*

**Meaning:** Only those, for whom Self-realization evolves into complete, firm maturity become Brahman in themselves. Others, who only give scholarly discourses or write academic articles do not attain this stage.

Katha Upaniṣad says that

नायमात्मा प्रवचनेन लभ्यो ।

*Nayamātmā pravacanen labhyo / (1.2.23)*

- Only a verbal or theoretical scholar does not gain the knowledge of Ātman.

When a seeker consistently conducts practices such as control of the mind (Śama, शम), control of the organs (Dama, दम) etc., he gains the grace of Sadguru, which ultimately results in complete maturity of the thought (Nididhyāsana) that 'I am Brahman'. After firm, steady, mature Self-realization, the theoretical knowledge becomes inconsequential for the person himself. However, he nurtures the knolwedge purely for educating and leading others on the same path of Self-realization.

Some people merely discuss the theoretical aspects of Brahman without putting them into practice. They crave for worldly pleasures, sink in the darkness of ignorance and go through the life-death cycle over and over again.

St. Jñāneśwara describes the enlightened people as those, who survive the ocean of worldly pleasures. When a person attains the firm, final, unchanging realization that 'I am Pure Bliss (not dependent on anything or anyone)', then the craving and pursuit of worldly pleasures automatically comes to an end.

## Importance of Self-realization

कुशला ब्रह्मवार्तायां वृत्तिहीनाः सुरागिणः ।
तेऽप्यज्ञानतया नूनं पुनरायान्ति यान्ति च ॥ १३३ ॥

*Kuśala Brahmavārtāyāṁ vṛttihīnāḥ surāginaḥ /*
*Te'pya jñānatayā nūnaṁ punarāyānti yānti ca // 133 //*

**Meaning:** Those, who are adept at discussions but do not realize Brahman may be very senior or superior in the theoretical knowledge. However, they also get born (and die) again and again like ignorant people for sure.

निमेषार्धं न तिष्ठन्ति वृत्तिं ब्रह्ममयीं विना ।
यथा तिष्ठन्ति ब्रह्माद्याः सनकाद्याः शुकादयः ॥ १३४ ॥

*Nimeṣārdhaṁ na tiṣṭanti vṛttiṁ Brahmamayiṁ vinā /*
*Yadā tiṣṭanti Brahmādyaḥ Sanakādyāḥ Śukādayaḥ // 134 //*

**Meaning:** Those who meditate on Brahman in this manner should not remain even a single moment without the thought of Brahman. They should continue their lives like Brahmadeva, Sanaka, Shuka and other such enlightened sages.

St. Jñānaśwara propounds the same in his treatise -

बुद्धीनिष्ठे आत्मज्ञान । ब्रह्मरूप भावी आपणा आपण ।
ब्रह्मनिष्ठा राखे पूर्ण । तत्परायण अहर्निशी ॥

*Buddhiniṣthe Ātmajñāna / Brahmarūpa bhāvi āpaṇā āpaṇa /*
*Brahmaniṣṭha rakhe pūrṇa / Tatparāyaṇa aharnishi // (5.87)*

- A seeker first makes a firm resolve with the intellect that 'Ātman is separate from the body' and gains theoretical knowledge (Parokṣa Jnana, परोक्ष ज्ञान) of Brahman. He then meditates upon the thought that he is One with the non-dual Brahman. He establishes utmost, undeterring faith in Brahman and maintains it day and night.

## Cause and effect

**कार्ये कारणतायाता कारणे न हि कार्यता ।**

**कारणत्वं स्वतो गच्छेत्कार्याभावे विचारतः ॥ १३५ ॥**

*Kārye kāraṇatāyātā kāraṇe na hi kāryatā /*

*Kāraṇatvaṁ svato gacchetkārya bhāve vicārataḥ // 135 //*

**Meaning:** The nature of the cause is present in its effect. While, the nature of the effect is not present in the casue. Hence, logic dictates that in the absence of effect, the cause too does not exist in the form of a cause.

Taittirīya Upaniṣad says –

**यतो व इमानि भूतानि जायन्ते ।**

*Yato vā imāni bhutāni jāyante / (3.1.1)*

- That from which these beings are born (is Brahman).

Because we experience this world in the form of effect (Kārya, कार्य), there must be a cause or reason (Brahman) behind its appearance.

However, from the perspective of Brahman, the effect (in the form of world) does not exist. Even if the visible world (Dṛśya, दृश्य) comes to an end, its cause - Brahman continues to exist. Therefore, by reasoning we can conclude that Brahman is perceived as the world in the form of effect. Even if the world (effect) disappears and the causal part of Brahman comes to an end, Brahman remains established in its very own Pure nature.

## Changeless, immutable Brahman

अथ शुद्धं भवेद्वस्तु यद्वै वाचामगोचरम् ।
द्रष्टव्यं मृद्घटेनैव दृष्टान्तेन पुनः पुनः ॥ १३६ ॥

*Atha śuddhaṁ bhavedvastu yadvai vācāmagocaraṁ /*
*Draṣṭavyam mṛdghatenaiva dṛṣṭantena punaḥ punaḥ // 136 //*

**Meaning:** Then Pure Brahman, that cannot be described by speech, alone remains. This should be understood repeatedly with the example of clay and pot.

Taittirīya Upaniṣad describes Brahman as -
यतो वाचो निवर्तन्ते अप्राप्य मनसा सह ।
*Yato vāco nivartante aprāpya manasā saha / (Tai. Up. 2.9.1)*

- The mind and speech return from it, since they are unable to understand or describe it.

This can be best understood with the example of clay and pot. If the name, form and color of a pot is sublated (in thoughts), then the clay alone remains. If a pot is broken, then it can be seen in the form of original clay. However, we cannot do the same with our body. St. Rāmadāsa describes the body as a collection of many elements such as earth, wind, fire etc. These transient (Māyic, मायिक) elements can be discarded in thoughts one by one to discover the real Self. If the three bodies (gross, subtle, causal) are refuted in meditation, then one can reach their illuminor Ātman. One can understand the relationship of illuminor-illumined (Prakāśaka-Prakāśya) between Ātman and three bodies. Illuminor Ātman is sentient, while illumined bodies are insentient in nature. In the end, the seeker can realize that I am the illuminor, Self-effulgent Ātman. The same concept can be understood with the example of nut-bolts and iron, ornaments and gold. One should learn to see only one iron among the wide variety of nuts and bolts and see only gold in various ornaments.

## The importance of spiritual practice

**अनेनैव प्रकारेण वृत्तिर्ब्रह्मात्मिका भवेत् ।**
**उदेति शुद्धचित्तानां वृत्तिज्ञानं ततः परम् ॥ १३७ ॥**

*Anenaiva prakāreṇa vṛttirbrahmātmika bhavet /*
*Udeti śuddha cittānāṁ vṛttijñānaṁ tataḥ param // 137 //*

**Meaning:** With this consistent practice alone, the seeker with pure mind gradually becomes aware of Ātman and later becomes completely One with Ātman.

Cidābhāsa and Ātman are originally one and the same. In meditation, when Vṛitti discards all other elements and becomes One with Ātman, there is no need to gain any separate knowledge. The knowledge of Ātman is ever-attained and ever-available. We are not aware of it only because it is covered by ignorance. One does not gain the knowledge of Ātman. It is revealed as soon as the cover of ignorance is removed or eradicated. Ignorance is removed when the subtle mind remains absorbed in Brahman and eventually disappears completely. The removal of cover of ignorance from Ātman is called as Vṛttivyāptī (वृत्तिव्याप्ती). As soon as this cover is removed, Cidābhāsa (Reflected Consciousnes) automatically merges into Brahman (Pure Consciousness). A seperate effort is not required to achive this. [Refer verse 109].

## Anvaya and Vyatireka

कारणं व्यतिरेकेण पुमानादौ विलोकयेत् ।
अन्वयेन पुनस्तद्धि कार्ये नित्यं प्रपश्यति ॥ १३८ ॥

*Kāraṇaṁ vyatirekeṇa pumānādou vilokayet /*
*Anvayena punastaddhi kārye nityaṁ prapaśyati // 138 //*

**Meaning:** The seeker should first perform the spiritual practice of refutation (Vyatireka, व्यतिरेक) and then realize the Self with the practice of seeing continuance (Anvaya, अन्वय). The Self is always present in the nature of the effect.

Vyatireka is the spiritual practice, where each element is refuted or negated in the mind. For example, 'this (mind) is not Brahman, this (intellect) is not Brahman' etc. In this method, one should think that all worldly objects and people are transient, illumined and insentient in nature. The following verse in Upaniṣad is the very foundation of this method -

नेति नेति ।

*Neti Neti / (Bru. Up. 2.3.6)*

- (Brahman is) not this, not this etc.

Once this spiritual practice evolves and matures completely, one sees the continuous presence of Brahman everywhere in all elements. Upaniṣad says -

**सर्वं खल्विदं ब्रह्म ।**

*Sarvaṁ khalvidaṁ Brahman | (Chan. Up. 3.14.1)*

- Everything is verily Brahman.

After Self-realization, one should look at every object in the manner – 'this too is Brahman, that too is Brahman' etc. This is the practice of Anvaya, where one sees the oneness and continuity of Brahman everywhere including himself.

St. Jñāneśwara says - Brahman equally pervades all sentient and insentient entities in the world.

The universe is divided into sentient and insentient entities for better understanding. However, Brahman pervades both types of entities equally.

As long as we perceive the world as real, Vedānta says (for beginners) that it consists of sentient and insentient entities. This is the language of 'false attribution' (Adhyāropa, अध्यारोप). The belief that the world exists for real is subsequently refuted (Apavāda, अपवाद) as seeker evolves in his spiritual pursuit. Everything is verily Brahman (Sarvaṁ Khalvidaṁ Brahman, सर्वं खल्विदं ब्रह्म) is the language of Apavāda. Both Adhyāropa-Apavāda lead the seeker towards Self-realization. The word 'everything' itself indicates the effect (KāryaBrahma). Seeker can progressively think in the following manner -

- Kārya-Brahma (कार्यब्रह्म): Brahman as the effect in the form of the world.
- Kāraṇa-Brahma (कारणब्रह्म): Brahman as the cause.
- Kārya-Kāraṇatita Śuddha Brahma (कार्यकारणातीत शुद्ध ब्रह्म): Pure Brahman that transcends both cause and effect.

The words Kāraṇa (कारण, cause) is relative to the Kārya (कार्य, effect). The seeker should gain the firm knowledge and belief that Pure Brahman transcends and exists irrespective of both cause and effect. That Pure Brahman is verily the nature of real I or Self.

A pot (effect, Kārya) consists of clay (cause, Kāraṇa), however, clay does not consist of a pot. Hence, clay exists whether pot exists or not. Thus, either way, one can verily see the clay. While looking at different pots, one may initially refute sizes, colors and shapes by thinking that 'this (size) is not clay, this (color) is not clay etc.' (Vyatireka, व्यतिरेक)'. Eventually as one matures, he can think that 'this (pot) is clay, this too is clay etc.' (Anvaya, अन्वय). Anvaya consists of thinking about clay while looking at all pots. Apavāda consists of refuting names-forms of pots in mind and focusing on only clay.

## Seeing the effect in the cause

**कार्ये हि कारणं पश्येत्पश्चात्कार्यं विसर्जयेत् ।**
**कारणत्वं स्वतो नश्येदवशिष्टं भवेन्मुनिः ॥ १३९ ॥**

*Kārye hi kāraṇaṁ paśyetpaścatkāryaṁ visarjayet |*
*Kāraṇatvaṁ swato nashyedavaśiṣṭam bhāvetmuniḥ || 139 ||*

**Meaning:** One should instinctively see the cause in all effects and then dissolve all effects (in thoughts). What remains is verily the real nature of the Self.

Millions of universes, infinite sentient species and all transactions are categorized as effect (Kārya, कार्य). Katha Upnishad says that -

नित्यम् अनित्यानाम् चेतनश्चेतनानाम् ।

*Nityam anityānām cetanaścetanānām | (2.2.13)*

- (Brahman is) the constant in all that is changing, and consciousness in all that is sentient or insentient. [Yet it is detached from everything.]

Brahman is the sentient root cause of the universe and pervades everything completely. In one of the rituals of Hinduism, a person picks up handful of water from river and dedicates it to the river again. Similarly, one should look at the cause, which verily exists in the form of effect, and make it disappear it back in the cause again. Later, what remains as the (so called) principle root cause (Kāraṇa, कारण), is the very own, ever-available, ever-existent, objective and immutable real Self of the seeker.

## Nididhyāsana of the real Self

भावितं तीव्रवेगेन यद्वस्तु निश्चयात्मना ।

पुमांस्तद्धि भवेच्छीघ्रं ज्ञेयं भ्रमरकीटवत् ॥ १४० ॥

*Bhāvitam tīvravegena yadvastu niścayātmana |*

*Pumānstaddhi bhavecchīghraṁ jñeyaṁ bhramarakīṭavat || 140 ||*

**Meaning:** A seeker who meditates upon an object with unwavering concentration and firm belief, becomes that object himself, just like a larva who becomes a wasp (after intent concentration).

This is the last and most subtle stage in spiritual pursuit. This is a practice that belongs to Rājayoga (राजयोग), which is the path of Knowledge described by Ādi Śaṅkarācārya in this treatise. It is different from the techniques of Samādhi (Dṛśyanuviddha - दृश्यानुविद्ध, Shabdānuviddha - शब्दानुविद्ध) described in the text of Dṛk Dṛśya Viveka. The ultimate stage of Self-realization is the same in all these techniques, which is evident in all practices of Kevala Advaita (Pure Non-duality).

Butterfly first exists in the form of larva. It intently thinks about its future form all the time. Eventually it evolves into butterfly. This example is used to illustrate a technique of meditation. The larva of Aham (I, अहं) should intently and uninterruptedly meditate upon the butterfly of Saha (सः, that principle of Brahman). Eventually the 'I' should dissolve and only 'Saha' or Brahman should remain. Only Brahman is Absolute, Pure Existence (Sat, सत्), while everything else has relative (dependent) existence. What should 'remain' at the end of meditation, is the only real, eternal Truth (Satya), while everything else that is refuted or discarded in meditation is transient, illusive and Māyic in nature.

## Anvaya (sameness in everything)

अदृश्यं भावरूपञ्च सर्वमेतत् चिदात्मकम् ।
सावधानतया नित्यं स्वात्मानं भावयेद्बुधः ॥ १४१ ॥

*Adṛśyam bhāvarūpañca sarvametat cidātmākam /*
*Sāvadhānatayā nityaṁ swātmānaṁ bhāvayedbudhaḥ // 141 //*

**Meaning:** A discerning seeker should carefully think about all perceivable and non-perceivable aspects, and conclude that everything is ultimately his real Self, Pure Consciousness (Ātman).

One who has pure and quiet mind, appropriate knowledge of Vedāntic scriptures and has earned the grace of Sadguru may be called as a discerning seeker. Detached person is naturally calm in nature. Detachment is the very nature of renunciation (Vairāgya, वैराग्य). St. Rāmadāsa says -

स्वरूपी जे सावधपण । तेचि ज्ञानाचे लक्षण ॥

*Svarūpi je sāvadhapaṇa / teci jñānāce lakṣāṇa / (PanchaSamasi)*

- The indication of real Knowledge is careful attentiveness to one's own Self (Ātman).

This is also called Pure Awareness or Pure Consciousness.

## The World (effect) should be dissolved in its cause

दृश्यं ह्यदृश्यतां नीत्वा ब्रह्माकारेण चिन्तयेत् ।
विद्वान्नित्यसुखे तिष्ठेद्धिया चिद्रसपूर्णया ॥ १४२ ॥

*Druśyam hyadṛśyatām nitvā Brahmākāreṇa cintayet /*
*Vidvānnityasukhe tiṣṭheddhiyā cidrasapūrṇayā // 142 //*

**Meaning:** By ensuring that the perceivable world disappears in imperceivable Brahman, a discerning seeker should consistently think that everything is only Brahman (and nothing else). He should then dwell in the supreme joy and Pure Bliss which is the nectar of Pure Consciousness.

The world disappears in deep-sleep and Samādhi. An enlightened person is able to sublate (Badha) the world in the waking state. He conducts his external life in an ordinary manner, while internally remains soaked in his own Self, Brahman. This itself is called as Bādha-Samādhi. Ādi Śaṅkarācārya and all enlightened saints did enormous work for the society by maintaining the state of Bādha Samādhi. They rejoiced in the eternal, uninterrupted flow of Pure Bliss. They could pledge themselves for leading others on the path of Pure Bliss.

Even when one understands that mirage is but an illusion, he continues to see the water, which does not exist in reality. Similarly, an enlightened person continues to perceive and transact with the world just like before the attainment of Knowledge of Brahman. However, he knows for sure that the world is not real. It is but an appearance. Māṇḍūkya Kārikā says -

ज्ञाते द्वैतम् न विद्यते ।

*Jñāte dvaitaṁ na vidyāte | (1.18)*

- An enlightened person does not see the duality.

This means that the perception of reality in the diversified appearance of the world comes to an end. However, the multiplicity itself does not end. St.

Vidyāranya Swāmi says in his treatise Pañcadashi, that one continues to see the duality even after enlightenment, however it is invalidated completely.

## The relationship between Rājayoga and Hathayoga

एभिरङ्गैः समायुक्तो राजयोग उदाहृतः ।

किञ्चित्पक्वकषायाणां हठयोगेन संयुतः ॥ १४३ ॥

*Ebhiraṅgaiḥ samāyukto Rājayoga udāhṛtaḥ |*

*Kincidpakvakaṣayānām Haṭhayogena saṅyuthaḥ || 143 ||*

**Meaning:** Thus, Rājayoga has been described with these (fifteen) aspects (explained earlier in verses 100-134). Those who are not completely detached from worldly matters, should combine this Rājayoga with the practice of Hathayoga.

Rājayoga (the path of Vedāntic Knowledge) is the best practice for those seekers who have perfected internal detachment from the worldly matters, since it involves sharp intellect and deep-thinking capacity. The ultimate detachment (Vairāgya) is that, when one even forgets that 'I am detached'. Being detached becomes his instinctive, effortless nature. It is called as Guṇagandha Vairāgya.

Those who are not detached should practice Prāṇayama as described in Hathayoga. They should resolutely put a leash on the wavering mind and establish the mind in Pure Consciousness (Ātman). An alert, vigilant and honest seeker knows his own level of detachment. He should agree with his own inner voice and perform the spiritual practice accordingly. Here, this verse guides the seeker to support Rājayoga that is mainly an intellectual practice with Hathayoga, which is predominantly a physical practice.

## The glory of Rājayoga

**परिपक्वं मनो येषां केवलोऽयं च सिद्धिदः ।**

**गुरुदैवतभक्तानां सर्वेषां सुलभो भवेत् ॥ १४४ ॥**

*Paripakvaṁ mano yeṣāṁ kevalo'yaṁ ca siddhidaḥ /*

*Gurudaivatabhaktānāṁ sarveṣāṁ sulabho bhāvet // 144 //*

**Meaning:** Rājayoga alone leads the seeker with purified mind towards Mokṣa (liberation). Those who are dedicated to Sadguru and God can tread the path of Rājayoga easily.

Purity, stability and calmness of the mind, unconditional surrender to Sadguru and worshipping the God have utmost importance in the pursuit of Mokṣa. Selfless actions as described in scriptures, lead to purification of the mind, and selfless worship leads to calmness of the mind. Utmost faith leads to worship of the God, while supreme fortune results in surrender to Sadguru. Texts written by luminary saints provide appropriate guidance for performing action and worship that is necessary for attaining Mokṣa. Their guidance can be easily followed even in the modern era.

St. Tukārāma has prescribed following actions for seekers of Mokṣa -

- Do not crave for the wealth that belongs to others
- Completely refrain from infidelity
- Chant the name of God
- Nurture faith in the guidance of enlightened saints
- Follow the path of truth

These and similar compositions give us the idea of actions and worship prescribed by saints. Selfless worship of God has enormous importance for attaining Mokṣa. All scholars of Vedānta have prescribed worship in some form. E.g. St. Sureśvarācārya, the author of Naiṣkarmyasiddhi and St. Sarvadnyātmāmuni, the author of Sankṣepa Śāriraka, have invoked and bowed to Lord Śri Viśṇū in the beginning and end of their respective treatises. St. Jñāneśwara says that chanting a Mantra gives a new lease of life (Sanjivani) to the practice of Samādhi. Meeting Sadguru, earning his grace, nurturing firm allegiance to Sadguru, following his orders, serving him, resolutely performing spiritual practices are promoted by saints and sages in many ways. One who earns or gains these qualities is a highly fortunate seeker.

When these rare qualities come together, the seeker experiences the glory of Rājayoga. Selfless actions and worship lead to the grace of God, which later result into the grace of the scriptures, Sadguru and ultimately the grace of Ātman. Let us all pray that may we all find and dwell in the company of such fortunate, enlightened saints!

|| श्रीकृष्णार्पणमस्तू ||